THE ELEVENTH HOUR

JESUS IS COMING... SOON!

Harold Collins

ISBN-13: 9781234567890
ISBN-10: 1477123456

Cover design by: Art Painter
Library of Congress Control Number: 2018675309
Printed in the United States of America

To my beautiful wife Selam and my sister Darlyn who is always in my corner. To my best friend Jeffrey who has been a great friend. And to Mollie who was a great friend throughout the darkest days and of course thank you Jesus for loving me and giving your life for me. Thank you Holy Spirit for giving me the words to write this book, and thank You for teaching me your Truth.

These things have I written unto you that believe on the name of the Son of God, that you may know that you have eternal life, and that you may believe on the name of the Son of God. He that has the Son has life and he that has not the Son of God has not life.

1 JOHN 5:13&12

CONTENTS

PREFACE

The Word of God is amazing!
A preacher once said, "This Bible that I hold in my hand is only a little more than an inch thick....

But it's A MILE DEEP!"

Truer words have never been spoken.

> *We are assured that, "No prophecy of the scripture is of any private interpretation. Because the prophecy came not in old time by the will of man, but holy men of God spoke (and wrote) as they were moved by the Holy Spirit." 2 Peter 1:20-21.*

In other words, God is the author of the scriptures.

> *"Eye has not seen, nor ear heard, neither have entered into the heart of man, the things which God has prepared for them that love Him. But God has revealed them to us by His Spirit: for the Spirit searches all things, yes, the DEEP things of God." 1 Corinthians 2:9-10.*

The Spirit of God reveals the spiritual aspects of God's word.

> *"For what man knows the things of a man, except by the spirit of man which is in him. Likewise, the things of God*

no man knows, but by the Spirit of God. Now we have received not the spirit of the world, but the Spirit which is of God: that we might know the things that are freely given to us of God."

"But the natural man receives not the things of the Spirit of God: for they are foolishness to him: neither can he know them, because THEY ARE SPIRITUALLY DISCERNED." 1 Corinthians 2:11-12, 14.

The Bible is a spiritual book written by men who were "carried along" by the Spirit of God and can be revealed to us by that same Spirit.

> The longer I live, and the more I study, the more I realize just how little I really know about God's Word.

My hope is that by sharing insights and revelations of God's Word that the reader may come to the same realization as I ... of JUST HOW AWESOME GOD REALLY IS!

Please pray and ask God to reveal these insights to you as you read, THE ELEVENTH HOUR, JESUS IS COMING... SOON!

INTRODUCTION

We are living in the last days of this world as we know it. All creation is a witness; events in the heavens and on the earth testify to this fact.

The world's religions also testify to the end of all things as we understand them. Even the secularists and atheists think that this world cannot sustain itself because humans are polluting it. The best scientific minds among us agree that we are destroying our habitation at an alarming rate.

These facts force us to ask some hard questions.

How much longer?

When will all these things as we know them, cease to exist?

The Mayan civilization sought to answer these questions with their calendar that expired on December 21st, 2012. We know that that date was wrong however because December 21st, 2012, came and went without much fanfare.

William Miller was studying the time prophecies of the book of Daniel early in the 19th century and concluded that the end of all things and Christ's return would occur in the year 1844... he was also mistaken, but the movement he began evolved into the founding of the 7th Day Adventist church.

Hospitals throughout the United States of America have been founded by the 7th Day Adventists, such as Loma Linda in California, Huguley in Texas, and some 50 others.

The point is: God can use even misguided error for good.

This "misguided error" may have even been at the hand of God to bring about much good and blessing. Read the story of Joseph culminating in Genesis 50:20.

Joseph's brothers wanted to kill him but instead sold him into slavery. However, their plans ultimately backfired when Joseph was promoted to Egypt's 2nd in command where he wisely stores up grain in 7 years of bountiful harvest so that many thousands could be saved in the coming 7 years of drought. It is in this context that Joseph told his brothers:

> *"But as for you, you thought evil against me; but God meant it unto good, to bring to pass, as it is this day, to save many people alive." Genesis 50:20.*

Of course, I realize that some, maybe even most reading this book, have been taught that all creation came about by no creative design, but by happenstance. That eons, and eons ago, in a pool of amino acids and proteins, the first one celled organism crawled out of this "primordial ooze" then through the process of Natural selection and survival of the fittest, all that we have come to know, which is all life, evolved. This concept is what our schools in the United States of America teach.

But think about it. Do you honestly believe that you and a housefly have a common ancestor?

Do you honestly believe that a duck billed platypus and you have a common ancestor in the tree of life?

If so, then where are the fossils of the "transitional species?" In other words, where is the half fly / half man fossil?

Or the half man / half platypus fossil? THEY DON'T EXIST.

Creation itself points to a Creator. There is intelligent design and order to the universe.

Be honest with yourself. Can you behold the magnificence of a starry night and not feel that something greater than yourself exists?

The ancient writings we call the Bible says:

> *"The fool says in his heart, "There is no God..." Psalm 14:1.*

> *"The heavens declare the glory of God and the sky proclaims His handiwork." Psalm 19:1.*

> *"The earth is the LORD'S and the fullness thereof, the world and those who dwell therein..." Psalm 24:1.*

So, are we to believe that there is no God?

I choose to believe in my heart of hearts that He does exist. I hope that you believe that too.

> *"But without faith it is impossible to please Him; for he that comes to God must believe that He is, and that He is a rewarder of those who diligently seek Him..." Hebrews 11:6.*

With the mindset that there is a Creator, and that the Creator of all things knows the end of all things and when it will be, this book will answer the questions posed earlier.

How much longer?

When will all these things as we know them cease to exist?

Understanding that there is a Creator and that He wants us to be prepared for the end of things as we know them; we will find the answers to these questions mentioned in the Word of God, which is the Bible.

> *"For the LORD GOD does nothing without revealing His secret to His servants the prophets." Amos 3:7*

God will, and does give us warning, instruction, correction, and wisdom through His Word and His prophets. The problem is: we are hard-headed and don't want to listen.

> *"The kings of the earth set themselves and the rulers take counsel together, against the LORD, and against His anointed saying, "Let us burst their bands apart and cast away their cords from us..." Psalm 2:2-3.*

There is nothing new under the sun. Mankind has rejected their Creator for millennia, but the wise will hear. Therefore, be warned. The end of all things as we know them is at hand. The time period (or, dispensation) for this existence is about to expire.

2031 Is The Year Of Expiration.

Milk at the grocery store has an expiration date... So does this world. The difference is that milk has a DAY of expiration. This world has only a year.

> *"But concerning that day and hour no one knows, not even the angels of heaven nor the Son, but the Father only." Matthew 24:36*

Do not be confused on this point. I do not know the day or the hour, or even the year. You see, Jesus, speaking of the end of the age said,

> *"Except those days should be shortened, there should no flesh be saved: but for the elect's sake those days shall be shortened." Matthew 24:22*

2031 is just the end of the "time allotted" or "determined." "Those Days" will be shortened.

In the next passage of Scripture, notice and put emphasis in the distinction that Paul is making between us / we, and they / them / those....

> *"Now concerning the times and seasons brethren, YOU yourselves know perfectly that the day of the LORD so comes as a thief in the night. For when THEY say, "Peace and safety" then sudden destruction comes upon THEM, as labor pains upon a pregnant woman. And THEY shall not escape. But YOU, BRETHREN, are not in darkness, that that day should overtake YOU as a thief. YOU are all the children of light, and the children of the day: WE are not of the night nor of darkness. Therefore, let US not sleep as do OTHERS; but let US watch and be sober. For THEY that sleep sleep in the night; and THEY that be drunken are drunken in the night, but let US, who are of the day, be sober, putting on the breastplate of faith and love; and for a helmet, the hope of salvation. For God has not appointed US to wrath, but to obtain salvation by our LORD Jesus Christ, who died for US, that whether WE wake or sleep WE should live together with Him." 1 Thessalonians 5:1-10.*

Sudden destruction will come upon THEM... (unbelievers, children of darkness).

Sudden destruction will not come upon US...

> *"Behold, I show you a mystery; We shall not all die, but we shall all be changed, in a moment, in the twinkling of an eye, at the LAST TRUMPET; for the trumpet shall sound, and the dead shall be raised incorruptible, and we shall be changed. For this corruptible must put on incorruption, and this mortal must put on immortality. So, when this corruptible shall have put on incorruption and this mortal shall have put on immortality, then shall be brought to pass the saying that is written, Death is swallowed up in victory. O death, where is your sting? O grave, where is your victory?" 1 Corinthians 15:51-55.*

The Last Trumpet Is Coming!

CHAPTER 1

THE WAVE SHEAF

"And the LORD spoke to Moses saying, "Speak to the children of Israel and say to them, Concerning the feasts of the LORD which you shall proclaim to be Holy Convocations, These are My Feasts: In the fourteenth day of the first month at sundown is the LORD'S Passover, and the next day starts the Feast of Unleavened Bread and that day which is the 15th day, is a High Day Sabbath and you shall have a Holy Convocation... and seven days later on the 22nd it is a High Day Sabbath and you shall have a Holy Convocation." Leviticus 23:1-2, 4-9.

The Passover observance was instituted by God as a deliverance of Israel from bondage in Egypt and eventually as a memorial, the Feast of Unleavened Bread became synonymous with the Passover.

Since the Passover and Feast of Unleavened Bread were comprised of 8 consecutive days there is always a weekly Sabbath contained therein. (Which starts at sundown Friday and ends at sundown Saturday).

It is this weekly Sabbath (Saturday) and the next day which is the 1st day of the week (Sunday) that God is referring to when He commands Moses saying,

"Speak to the children of Israel and say to them When

you come into the land which I give to you, and shall reap the HARVEST thereof, then you shall bring a SHEAF of the FIRSTFRUITS of your HARVEST to the PRIEST: And he shall WAVE THE SHEAF before the LORD; to be ACCEPTED FOR YOU: ON THE DAY AFTER THE SABBATH THE PRIEST SHALL WAVE IT." (Sunday). Leviticus 23:10-11.

So, the day after the 7th day Sabbath is the 1ST day of the week … Sunday … It was exactly on this Sunday during the feast of unleavened bread that Mary Magdalene came early in the morning to Jesus' tomb. John 20:1.

"The first day of the week comes Mary Magdalene early, when it was still dark to the sepulchre and saw the stone taken away from the tomb. Then she ran and came to Simon Peter, and the other disciple whom Jesus loved, and said to them, "They have taken away the Lord out of the sepulchre and we don't know where they have laid him." "Peter therefore went forth and that other disciple and came to the sepulchre. So, they ran both together and the other disciple did outrun Peter and came first to the sepulchre. And he, stooping down, and looking in, saw the linen clothes lying; but he did not go in. Then came Simon Peter following him, and went into the sepulchre, and saw the linen clothes lying, AND THE NAPKIN THAT WAS ABOUT HIS HEAD, not lying with the linen clothes, but WRAPPED TOGETHER in a place by itself." John 20:1-7.

What beautiful imagery of the only "SIGN" given to that generation!

"Then certain of the Scribes and Pharisees said, "Master we would like to see a sign from you. But Jesus answered

them saying, "An evil and adulterous generation seek after a sign; and there shall be no sign given to it EXCEPT the sign of the prophet Jonah. For as Jonah was 3 days and 3 nights in the whale's belly so shall the Son of Man be 3 days and 3 nights in the heart of the earth." Matthew 12:39-40

"Now the LORD had prepared a great fish to swallow up Jonah. And Jonah was in the belly of the fish 3 days and 3 nights. Then Jonah prayed to the LORD his God out of the fish's belly, and said, "I cried by reason of my affliction unto the LORD, and He heard me, out of the belly of the pit, I cried, and You heard my voice. For You cast me into the deep, into the midst of the seas; and the floods compassed me about and all Thy billows and waves PASSED OVER me. Then I said, "I am cast out of Your sight; yet I will look again toward Your Holy Temple. The waters compassed me about, even to the soul; the depth closed me round about, THE WEEDS WERE WRAPPED ABOUT MY HEAD." Jonah 1:17-2:5.

What an awesome detail given in John 20! That the linen wrapped around our Saviors head in the tomb was foreshadowed by the sea weeds wrapped around Jonah's head in the belly of the great fish! God is so awesome!

Notice also, the language the prophet Jonah uses in describing the billows and waves... how they "PASSED OVER" him. I think he was describing his protection much like the children of Israel's protection from the destroying angel at the first Passover.

"Then the disciples went away again to their own home. But Mary stood without at the sepulchre weeping: and as she wept, she stooped down and looked in the sepulchre,

and saw 2 angels in white sitting, one at the head, the other at the feet, where the body of Jesus had lain. And they said to her, "Woman, why are you crying?" She said to them, "Because they have taken away my Lord and I don't know where they have laid Him. And when she had said this, she turned and saw Jesus standing but did not know that it was Jesus. Jesus said, "Woman why are you crying whom do you seek?" She SUPPOSING HIM TO BE THE GARDENER, said, "Sir, if you've taken Him from here, tell me where you have laid Him; and I will take Him away." John 20:10-15

Once again, what beautiful imagery!

Mary's vision was blurry because of tear swollen eyes, and looking at Jesus, she mistook Him for the gardener, because He is holding THE WAVE SHEAF IN HIS HAND!

The WAVE SHEAF symbolizes the first fruits of the HARVEST. Leviticus 23:10

"But now Christ is risen from the dead AND BECOME THE FIRSTFRUITS OF THEM THAT SLEPT. For since by man (Adam) came death, by Man (Jesus) came the resurrection of the dead. For as in Adam all die even in Christ shall all be made alive. But every man in his own order: CHRIST THE FIRSTFRUITS; afterward, they that are Christs at His coming." 1 Corinthians 15:20-23

Another fact which deserves mention here is the resemblance of the 2 angels, (one at the head and one at the feet, of where Jesus had laid) to the Mercy Seat.

"And you shall make two cherubims of gold, of beaten work shall you make them, in the two ends of the mercy

seat. And make one cherub on the one end and the other cherub on the other end: you shall make the cherubims ON THE TWO ENDS THEREOF." Exodus 25:18-19

Another interesting aspect of the wave sheaf imagery is that the Hebrew word translated: "sheaf"   is -OMER- and connotes a "heap" of grain, or measure... In other words, on Sunday morning during the Feast of Unleavened bread, the Israelites would bring not one little stalk of barley, but many stalks to comprise the handful... or WAVE SHEAF... the "FIRSTFRUITS OF THE HARVEST" symbolizing the resurrection of Christ, the FIRSTFRUITS OF THE HARVEST OF SOULS... THE RESURRECTION. And, since the Lord is awesome in the portrayal of the imagery, He resurrected many saints the help comprise the wave sheaf.

"And the graves were opened and many bodies of the saints which slept arose and came out of the graves after His resurrection and went into the holy city and appeared to many." Matthew 27:52-53

In John 20 the imagery continues:

"Jesus said to her, Mary. She turned herself and said to Him, Rabboni, which is to say, Master. Jesus said to her, TOUCH ME NOT, FOR I AM NOT YET ASCENDED TO MY FATHER, but go to my brethren and say to them, I ascend to My Father and your Father, to My God and your God." John 20:16-17

An important question needs to be answered at this point: Why did Jesus tell Mary NOT TO TOUCH HIM?

The answer is in the words immediately following the command to not touch Him... "

"For I am not yet ascended to my Father."

He had not yet ascended to the Father as the FIRSTFRUITS OF THE RESURRECTION to be ACCEPTED.

"Then you shall bring a sheaf of the first fruits of your harvest to the Priest: and He shall WAVE THE SHEAF before the LORD, TO BE ACCEPTED FOR YOU: on the day after the Sabbath (Sunday morning) the Priest shall wave it." Leviticus 23:10b-11

Had Mary touched Him she would have defiled the offering.

Every year, during the Passover/Feast of Unleavened Bread, the children of Israel brought a wave sheaf of the first fruits of their barley harvest not realizing the symbolism and extremely important implication for humanity.

"How much more shall the blood of Christ who through the eternal Spirit offered Himself WITHOUT SPOT to God, purge your conscience from dead works to serve the living God?" Hebrews 9:14

We have the advantage here in the 21st century of hindsight. We can look back at Old Testament Scripture and see, with the help of the Holy Spirit, the types, shadows, and figures of heavenly things.

Jesus ascended to the Father to present Himself as the first fruits of the resurrection without spot or blemish to be accepted for our redemption.

> *"Forasmuch as you know that you were not redeemed with corruptible things, as silver and gold, from your vain conversation received by tradition from your fathers, but with the precious blood of Christ, as a lamb without blemish and without spot." 1 Peter 1:18-19*

Another question arises: When did Jesus ascend to the Father to be accepted as the Wave Sheaf offering? Was it forty days later as described in Acts 1:9?

No, of course not. That would not fit the "type" of Leviticus 23:11.

Jesus told Mary not to touch Him early in the morning on Sunday. He also told her to go and tell His brethren that He was going to ascend to the Father. Later that evening, Jesus appeared to the brethren and showed them his hands and His side where He was pierced. Eight days later He told doubting Thomas to touch Him. John 20: 19-31

So, it is apparent that Jesus ascended to the Father to be accepted as the FIRSTFRUITS of the RESURRECTION on Sunday after speaking with Mary and before evening when He appeared to the disciples.

Jesus' cousin, John the Baptist, identified Jesus as the "Passover Lamb of God" as Jesus began His earthly ministry...

> *"Behold, the Lamb of God which takes away the sin of the world." John 1:29b*

Paul identified Jesus as the Passover Lamb of God as well:

> *"Purge out therefore the old leaven, that you may be a*

new lump, as you are unleavened. For even CHRIST OUR PASSOVER is sacrificed for us. Therefore, let us keep the feast, not with old leaven, neither with the leaven of malice and wickedness; but with the unleavened bread of sincerity and truth." 1Corinthians 5:7-8

From the very first Passover, the plan of redemption is foreshadowed by the blood of the lamb.

"Your lamb shall be without blemish... and the whole assembly of the congregation of Israel shall kill it and shall take the blood and strike it on the two side posts and on the upper door post of the houses... and the blood shall be to you for a token upon the houses where you are: and when I see the blood, I WILL PASS OVER YOU," Exodus 12: 5a,6b,7,13a.

Jesus Is Our Passover Lamb Of God.

Jesus Is The Wave Sheaf.

CHAPTER 2

THE ROCK

The children of Israel's deliverance from bondage in Egypt serves as an example to us today. Paul said,

> *"All these things happened to them for examples: and they are written for our warning, upon whom the ends of the world are come." 1Corinthians 10:11*

The language Paul uses here is very forceful. The Greek word for ensample/example means "a model (for imitation)" or "instance (for warning)."

> We have a choice, to use the Exodus as a model for imitation, or for a warning, dependent upon the choice we make.

The children of Israel were witnesses to the plagues that came upon the Egyptians and when Pharoah finally agreed to let them go, the LORD hardened Pharoah's heart once again and the entire Egyptian army pursued after the children of Israel, and they were afraid. But Moses said to the people,

> *"Fear NOT, stand still, and see the salvation of the LORD which He will show you today. For the Egyptians whom you have seen today, you shall see them again no more,*

forever. The LORD shall fight for you, and you shall hold your peace." Exodus 14:13-14

What great instruction for us today! FEAR NOT, STAND STILL, SHUT UP, AND WATCH THE LORD WORK!!

The LORD parted the Red Sea that day and the children of Israel were delivered through the water safely to the other side and the Egyptian army were all drowned in the sea. Exodus 14.

"And all the congregation of the children of Israel journeyed from the wilderness of SIN, after their journeys, according to the commandment of the LORD and camped in Rephidim: and there was no water for the people to drink. And because of this, the people complained to Moses and said, "Give us water that we may drink." And Moses said to them, "Why do you complain to me? Why do you tempt the LORD?" And the people thirsted there for water; and the people murmured against Moses, and said, "Why did you bring us up out of Egypt, to kill us and our children and our cattle with thirst?" And Moses cried unto the LORD saying, "What shall I do unto this people? They're almost ready to stone me!" And the LORD said to Moses, "Go on before the people, and take with you the elders of Israel and the ROD that you smote the river with and go. Behold, I will stand before you there upon the ROCK at HOREB, and you shall SMITE (strike) the ROCK, and there shall come water out of it, that the people may drink. And Moses did so in the sight of the elders of Israel." Exodus 17:1-6.

Once again, what beautiful imagery!

Paul speaking of the children of Israel said,

*"They all drank the same spiritual drink: for they drank
of that spiritual ROCK that followed them: AND THAT
ROCK WAS CHRIST." 1Corinthians 10:4.*

Jesus Himself continues this spiritual imagery,

*"Then He came to a city of Samaria, which is called
Sychar, near to the parcel of ground that Jacob gave to
his son Joseph. Now Jacob's well was there. Jesus, therefore, being wearied with His journey, sat on the well: and
it was about 12 o'clock noon. There came a woman of
Samaria to draw water and Jesus said to her, "Give me
something to drink." (For His disciples were gone away
into the city to buy food). Then the woman of Samaria
said to Him, "How is it that you, being a Jew, ask me to
give you a drink, I am a woman of Samaria, and the Jews
have no dealings with the Samaritans." Jesus answered
and said to her, "If you knew the gift of God, and Who it
is that said to you, give me something to drink; you would
have asked Him, and He would have given you LIVING
WATER." "Whosoever drinks of this water shall thirst
again: but whosoever drinks of the water that I shall give
him shall never thirst; but the water that I give him shall
be in him a well of water, springing up into everlasting
life." John 4:5-10,14.*

Jesus was, of course, speaking of the Holy Spirit. Remember, the
Scriptures are written by God Almighty who is SPIRIT.

*"God is SPIRIT: and they that worship Him must worship
Him in SPIRIT AND IN TRUTH." John 4:24*

Therefore, we must seek to understand a spiritual book written by a spiritual being, with the Spirit of God who lives in us… the Holy Spirit.

The Rock at Horeb is just one of many examples in the Bible that teaches a deeper spiritual reality than what is readily apparent on the surface… Remember, Paul said that the Rock is Christ and God told Moses to "SMITE" (strike) the Rock and it would give forth its water. (Which was a "type" or symbol of Christ's crucifixion and the water a "type" of the Holy Spirit).

Isaiah wrote:

> *"Surely He has borne our griefs and carried our sorrows: yet we did esteem Him stricken, SMITTEN OF GOD, and afflicted." Isaiah 53:4.*

Why is it important to point out the fact that God told Moses to SMITE the Rock and that this action represents the Crucifixion of Christ?

Several reasons, one being that you, as the reader, need to understand the spiritual aspects and meanings behind the events surrounding the Exodus, or you will not be able grasp spiritual realities presented in this book.

Another reason is so we can understand what happened later in Israel's journey which deals with the same scenario, the people were thirsty, and God used Moses to bring water from the ROCK, but this time with dramatic results concerning Moses.

> *"Then came the children of Israel, even the whole congregation, into the desert of ZIN in the first month (which just-so-happens to be the month of PASSOVER), and the people abode in Kadesh; and Miriam died there and was buried there. And there was no water for the congregation: and they gathered themselves together against Moses and against Aaron. And the people chode with*

Moses, and spoke, saying "Would God {rather} that we had died when our brethren died before the LORD! And why have you brought up the congregation of the LORD into this wilderness, that we and our cattle should die there? And why have you made us to come up out of Egypt, to bring us unto this evil place? It is no place of seed, or of figs, or of vines, or of pomegranates; neither is there any water to drink." And Moses and Aaron went from the presence of the assembly unto the door of the tabernacle of the congregation and they fell upon their faces: and the glory of the LORD appeared unto them. And the LORD spoke unto Moses, saying, "Take the rod, and gather the assembly together, you, and Aaron your brother and SPEAK UNTO THE ROCK BEFORE THEIR EYES; and it shall give forth HIS WATER, and you shall bring forth to them water out of the ROCK: so, you shall give the congregation and their beasts drink." Numbers 20:1-8

Notice that God tells Moses to take his rod but unlike before, He tells Moses to SPEAK TO THE ROCK BEFORE THEIR EYES...

The LORD is revealing part of the plan of salvation to the children of Israel (and to us as well) in that the ROCK has already been SMITTEN (type of Christ's crucifixion) and now all we need to do is SPEAK (PRAY) TO THE ROCK.

Notice also, that God calls the water, HIS WATER. (KJV)

"And Moses and Aaron gathered the congregation together before the ROCK, and he said to them, "Hear now you rebels; must we fetch you water out of this ROCK?And Moses lifted his hand, and with his rod he SMOTE THE ROCK... TWICE: and the water came out abundantly, and the congregation drank, and their beasts also." Numbers 20:10-11

Moses Disobeyed The Lord!

Instead of speaking to the ROCK he smote (hit) the ROCK... twice!

You see, the Exodus out of bondage from Egypt tells the salvation story in "type" or "shadow" for humanity. Moses messed up the lesson that GOD was teaching the children of Israel and ultimately, us. So, what punishment did Moses receive?

> "And the LORD spoke to Moses and Aaron, "Because you believed me not, to sanctify Me in the eyes of the children of Israel, therefore YOU SHALL NOT BRING THIS CONGREGATION INTO THE LAND WHICH I HAVE GIVEN THEM." (the "promised land"). Numbers 20:12.

> "And Moses went up from the plains of Moab unto the mountain of Nebo to the top of Pisgah, that is over against Jericho. And the LORD showed him all the land of Gilead, unto Dan, and all Naphtali, and the land of Ephraim and Manasseh and all the land of Judah, unto the sea, and the south, and the plain of the valley of Jericho, the city of palm trees, unto Zoar. And the LORD said unto him, "This is the land which I swore unto Abraham, unto Isaac, and unto Jacob saying, I will give it unto your seed: I have caused you to see it with your eyes, BUT YOU SHALL NOT GO OVER THERE." So, Moses the servant of the LORD died there in the land of Moab, according to the word of the LORD." Deuteronomy 34:1-5

Moses' death on the east side of the Jordan played into a spiritual reality that is not apparent unless you think about it.

If God had allowed Moses to lead the Children of Israel into the Promised Land, then the "type" or "shadow" of the greater spiritual reality that underlies the Exodus narrative, would have been broken...

Let me explain, Moses' name in the Hebrew language is "Mo-sheh" which means: "drawing out" (of the water), i.e., rescued.

Moses' successor's name: "Yah-shua" (Joshua), means: "Yahweh's Salvation." Joshua and Jesus have the same Hebrew name.

Joshua is the forerunner of Jesus and led the Children of Israel into their "Promised Land" just as Jesus leads us into the Kingdom of God... our "Promised Land."

> *"I will publish the name of the LORD: ascribe greatness unto our God. HE IS THE ROCK His work is perfect." Deuteronomy 32:3-4*

> *"The LORD is my ROCK and my fortress, and my deliverer; my God." Psalm 18:2*

> *"Unto you will I cry, O LORD my ROCK." Psalm 28:1*

> *"He only is my ROCK, and my SALVATION: He is my defense; I shall not be moved." Psalm 62:6*

Jesus spoke of the Spiritual reality and importance of the ROCK in His summation of the Sermon on the Mount...

> *"Therefore, whosoever hears these sayings of mine and does them, I will liken him a wise man which built his house upon a ROCK: the rain descended, and the floods*

came, the winds blew and beat upon that house; and it fell not: because it was founded upon a ROCK. And everyone that hears these sayings of mine, and does them not, shall be like a foolish man which built his house upon the sand: and the rain descended, and the floods came, and the winds blew and beat upon that house; and it fell: and great was the fall of it." Matthew 7:24-27

Jesus also spoke of this reality in His discourse to Peter and the disciples about the founding of the church:

"When Jesus came into the coasts of Caesarea Philippi, He asked His disciples, saying: Who do men say that I the Son of man am? And they said, some say that you are John the Baptist: some, Elijah; and others, Jeremiah or one of the prophets. He said to them, BUT WHO DO YOU SAY THAT I AM? And Simon Peter answered and said, you are the Christ, the Son of the living God. And Jesus answered and said to him, blessed are you Simon Bar-jona: for flesh and blood has not revealed it unto you, but My Father which is in heaven. And I say also unto you, that you are PETER, (Greek word: Petros meaning a piece of rock) and upon this ROCK (Greek word: Petra meaning a MASS OF ROCK{Jesus}) I will build my church and the gates of hell shall not prevail against it." Matthew 16:13-18

Jesus WAS NOT saying that He was founding the church upon Peter! No!

He WAS saying that the church is founded upon the ROCK OF OUR SALVATION... HIMSELF, JESUS CHRIST.

Remember to look at the context. The discourse was about who Jesus really is... Not Peter.

Peter himself wrote of this "Rock."

"Behold, I lay in Zion a chief corner STONE, elect, precious: and he that believes on Him shall not be confounded. Unto you therefore which believe He is precious: but unto them which be disobedient, the Stone which the builders rejected, the same is made the head of the corner, and a stone of stumbling and a Rock of offence, even to them which stumble at the word, being disobedient: whereunto also they were appointed. But you are a chosen generation, a royal priesthood, a holy nation, a peculiar people; that you should show forth the praises of Him who has called you out of darkness into HIS MARVELLOUS LIGHT." 1 Peter 2:6-9.

Jesus Is The Chief Corner Stone... Not Peter.

Moreover, brethren I would not that you should be ignorant, how that all our fathers were under the cloud and all passed through the sea; and were all BAPTIZED unto Moses int the cloud and in the sea; and did all eat the same spiritual meat (bread from heaven, Manna) and did all drink the same spiritual drink: for they drank of that spiritual ROCK that followed them; and that ROCK WAS CHRIST." 1Corinthians 10:1-4

Jesus Is The Rock.

CHAPTER 3

THE BREAD

J esus was born in Bethlehem which consists of two words: Beth = House, Lehem = Bread. He was born in the "House of Bread."

After Israel's miraculous delivery from bondage in Egypt, they were hungry and once again voiced their complaint to Moses.

> *"And they took their journey from Elim, and all the congregation of the children of Israel came into the wilderness of SIN, which is between Elim and Sinai, on the fifteenth day of the second month after their departing out of the land of Egypt. And the whole congregation of the children of Israel murmured against Moses and Aaron in the wilderness: And the children of Israel said to them, "When we were in the land of Egypt, we ate bread until we were full but now you have brought us into this wilderness to kill this whole assembly with hunger." "Then said the LORD unto Moses, "Behold, I will rain bread from heaven for you; and the people shall go out and gather a certain rate every day, that I may prove them whether they will walk in My law or not." "And the children of Israel saw it, they said to one another, "It is manna." (For they did not know what it was.) And Moses said to them, "This is the bread which the LORD has given you to eat." "And the house of Israel called the name thereof MANNA:*

and it was like Coriander seed." Exodus 16:1-4, 15a, 31a.

It is interesting to note at this point that the children of Israel were in the wilderness of "SIN" ... just as we are living in a sinful world.

Also, the Hebrew word translated "manna" is: MAN.

The scripture says that the manna (MAN) was like "coriander" seed.

The Hebrew word translated "coriander" is: GAD. The "A" in GAD is pronounced as the "A" in father which leads us to the pronunciation: GAWD. (GOD)

Once again, what beautiful imagery!

Who is the MAN/GOD?

Jesus, of course!

Jesus said, "Our fathers did eat manna in the desert; as it is written, He gave them bread from heaven to eat. Then Jesus said unto them, Verily, verily I say unto you, Moses gave you not that bread from heaven; but my Father gives you the true bread from heaven. For the bread of God is He which comes down from heaven and gives life unto the world. Then they said to Him, Lord, give us this bread. And Jesus said to them, I AM THE BREAD OF LIFE: He that comes to me shall never hunger; and he that believes on Me shall never thirst." John 6:31-35

"Verily, verily, I say unto you, He that believes on Me has everlasting life. I AM THAT BREAD OF LIFE. Your fathers did eat manna in the wilderness and are dead. This is the bread which comes down from heaven, that a man may eat thereof and not die. I AM THE LIVING BREAD which

came down from heaven: if any man eats this bread, he shall live forever: and the bread that I will give is My flesh which I will give for the life of the world. The Jews therefore strove among themselves, saying, "How can this man give us His flesh to eat?" Jesus said to them, "Verily, verily, I say to you, unless you eat the flesh of the Son of man, and drink His blood, you have no life in you. Whosoever eats My flesh, and drinks My blood has eternal life; and I will raise him up at the last day, for My flesh is meat indeed, and My blood is drink indeed. He that eats My flesh and drinks My blood, dwells in Me, and I in him. As the living Father has sent Me, and I live by the Father: so, he that eats Me, even he shall live by Me. This is that bread which came down from heaven: not as your fathers did eat manna and are dead: he that eats of this bread shall live forever." John 6:47-58

Living in the 21st century we have the advantage of hindsight. Put yourself for a moment back in the 1st century and imagine that you are witness to the words of Jesus... His words must have been very perplexing! Was He speaking of cannibalism? Has this Man lost His Mind?

I can only imagine the confusion His followers must have been experiencing!

God's provision for Israel in the wilderness is a reminder for us as well that God will provide the necessities of life. The manna was just one example. The shewbread is another.

Jesus said, "Take no thought for your life, what you shall eat, or what you shall drink; nor yet for your body, what you shall put on. Is not the life more than meat, and the body than clothes? Behold the fowls of the air: for they sow not, neither do they reap, nor gather into barns; yet your heavenly Father feeds them. Are you not much bet-

ter than they? Which of you by taking thought can add one cubit unto his stature? And why do you think about clothes? Consider the lilies of the field, how they grow; they toil not, neither do they spin: and yet I say unto you, even Solomon in all his glory was not arrayed like one of these. Wherefore, if God so clothe the grass of the field, which today is and tomorrow is cast into the oven, shall He not much more clothe you, O you of little faith? Therefore, take no thought, saying, "What shall we eat? Or what shall we drink? Or where will our clothes come from?" (For after all these things do the Gentiles seek:) for your Heavenly Father knows that you have need of all these things. But seek you first the kingdom of God, and all these things shall be added unto you." Matthew 6:25-33

God used Israel's trek in the wilderness for 40 years to teach them to rely upon Him for sustenance. He uses Israel as an example for us as well.

"Now these things were our examples, to the intent we should not lust after evil things, as they also lusted... Now all these things happened unto them for ensamples: and they are written for our admonition, upon whom the ends of the world are come." 1Corinthians 10:6, 11.

The word translated "admonition" is a Greek word that means: "mild rebuke or warning." It's the same word used in Titus 3:10. "A man that is a heretic after the first and second admonition (rebuke or warning) reject.

The word translated "ensamples" is a Greek word that means: "a sampler ("type"), i.e., a model (for imitation) or instance (for warning).

As covered already in Chapter 1, the Exodus from Egypt and the subsequent 40 years of wilderness wandering, serve as either an example, or a warning for us today.

My hope is that you can comprehend the spiritual realities (with the help of the Holy Spirit) presented in the Scriptures and that you are fully aware of the "type / antitype" method of God's teachings.

Jesus Is The Bread.

Jesus Is The Rock.

Jesus Is The Passover Lamb.

Jesus Is The Wave Sheaf.

For Centuries, the Children of Israel would kill a lamb on the 14th day of the first month of the Jewish Calendar to commemorate the very first Passover in which the destroying angel would "pass over" the houses which had the blood of the lamb on the door posts. (Exodus 12).

And on the 15th day of the first month the Children of Israel would have a "holy convocation" which was to be a "High Day" Sabbath. And 7 days later, they would have another "holy convocation' (holy gathering) which was also a "High Day" or special Sabbath in which no work was to be done. During the 7-day Feast of Unleavened Bread all leavening agents such as yeast would be removed from their homes to remember the haste in which they left Egypt.

In the New Testament era, Paul uses leaven in the metaphorical sense of "impurity" which must be purged out.

"Purge out therefore the old leaven, that you may be a new lump, as you are unleavened. For even Christ, our Passover is sacrificed for us: Therefore, let us keep the feast, not with old leaven, neither with the leaven of malice and wickedness; but with the unleavened bread of SINCERITY and TRUTH." 1Corinthians 5:7-8

These observances pointed FORWARD to the CROSS and Jesus, the lamb of God who takes away the sin of the world... He who was without blemish or spot.

A "new" observance was instituted by Jesus at what is called: The Last Supper.

"And as they were eating, Jesus took bread, and blessed it and broke it and gave it to the disciples and said, "Take, eat; this is My body." And He took the cup and gave thanks, and gave it to them, saying, "Drink you all of it; For this is My blood of the New Testament which is shed for many for the remission of sins." Matthew 26:26-28.

As already mentioned, the Old Testament observances pointed forward to the Cross. Now, Jesus was about to fulfill the "type" of the Passover Lamb and give His life on the Cross.

Paul said, "For I have received of the Lord that which also I delivered unto you, That the Lord Jesus the same night in which He was betrayed took bread: and when He had given thanks, He broke it and said, "Take and eat, this is My body which is broken for you: this do in REMEMBRANCE of Me. After the same manner also, He took the cup when He had drank saying, "This cup is the New Testament in My blood: this do you as often as you drink it, in REMEMBRANCE of Me. For as often as you eat this bread, and drink this cup, you do show the Lord's death till He come." 1Corinthians 11:23-26.

The Passover Lamb pointed FORWARD to the cross.

The "new" observance instituted by our Lord Jesus points "Backward" to the CROSS.

Jesus Is The Manna.

Jesus Is The Bread From Heaven.

CHAPTER 4

THE WAY

In the beginning God created the first man, Adam and his wife Eve to tend the Garden which was in Eden.

After the "fall" of man (by sinning) God cast them out of the Garden...

> *"So, He drove out the man; and He placed cherubim at the east of the Garden of Eden, and a flaming sword which turned every way, to guard THE WAY to the tree of life."*
> *Genesis 3:24*

The flaming sword which turned every "way" is a different Hebrew word than the word used for the "WAY" to the tree of life.

The Hebrew word "hapak" means: to overthrow, overturn, turn around, change...

The Hebrew word used for the "WAY" to the tree of life is: "DEREK" and means: way, path, route, road, journey, conduct, WAY OF LIFE...

The "WAY" to the tree of life was sacrificed on the altar of sin by the "first Adam."

The "WAY" to the tree of life was restored by the "Son of Man" the "second Adam."

"And he showed me a pure river of water of life, clear as crystal, proceeding out of the throne of God and of the Lamb. In the middle of the street of it and on either side of the river, was the tree of life, which bare twelve manner of fruits, and yielded her fruit every month and the leaves of the tree were for the healing of the nations." Revelation 22:1-2

In the Sermon on the Mount Jesus said.

"Enter by the narrow gate; for wide is the gate and broad is the WAY that leads to destruction, and there are many who go in by it. Because straight is the gate, and narrow is the WAY which leads to life, and few there be that find it." Matthew 7:13-14

Jesus paints a somewhat gloomy picture here. He makes it sound like most will not make it into the kingdom.

One of the wisest men who ever lived said,

"There is a WAY that seems right to a man, but the end thereof are the WAYS of death." Proverbs 14:12

The exact same verse is repeated in Proverbs 16:25. When the Bible repeats itself it is to place greater emphasis on what is being said.

Jesus also said in the Sermon on the Mount,

"Not everyone who says to me, Lord, Lord, shall enter into the kingdom of heaven; but he that does the will of my Father which is in heaven. Many will say to Me in that

day, Lord, Lord, have we not prophesied in your name? And in your name have cast out devils? And in your name done many wonderful works? Then I will profess to them, I never knew you: depart from Me, you that work iniquity." Matthew 7:21-23

Jesus says that these people think that they are saved, but they practice lawlessness, so they are not. They resemble the Pharisees and Sadducees. People who are self-righteous and relying on their works... These people think they are saved from destruction but do not know Him in their hearts.

Jesus was pressed by the Pharisees to answer this question:

"Teacher, which is the Great Commandment in the law?" Jesus said, "You shall Love the LORD your God with all your heart, with all your soul, and with all your mind. This is the first and Great Commandment. And the second is like it: You shall Love your neighbor as yourself..." On these two commandments hang all the law and the prophets." Matthew 22:37-40.

Paul said it like this:

"Owe no one anything except to Love one another: for he that loves another has fulfilled the law. For this: You shall not commit adultery, You shall not kill, You shall not steal, You shall not bear false witness, You shall not covet; and if there be any other commandment, it is briefly comprehended in this saying, namely, You shall Love Your Neighbor as yourself. Love works no ill to his neighbor; therefore, Love is the fulfilling of the law." Romans 13: 8-10.

If I Love my neighbor, I will not sleep with his wife or steal from

him or lie about him. Those are the "WAYS" of death. The wrong
path. The wrong journey.

Jesus said,

> *"I AM the WAY, the TRUTH, and the LIFE. No one comes to
> the Father except through Me." John 14:6.*

The Path to the Father, the "WAY" back to the Tree of
    Life, is only through Jesus.

*"He that enters not by the Door into the sheepfold but
climbs up some other way, the same is a thief and a rob-
ber. But He that enters in by the Door is the Shepherd of
the sheep. To Him the Porter opens; and the sheep hear
His voice: and He calls His own sheep by name and leads
them out. And when He puts forth His own sheep, He goes
before them, and the sheep follow Him because they know
His voice. And a stranger will they not follow but will flee
from him for they do not know the voice of strangers. This
parable Jesus spoke to them, but they did not understand
what the things were that He spoke. Then Jesus said to
them again surely, surely, I say to you I AM the Door of
the sheep. All that ever came before Me are thieves and
robbers, but the sheep did not hear them. I AM the Door. If
any man enters in, he shall be saved, and shall go in and
out and find pasture. The thief comes only to steal, kill
and to destroy. I have come that they might have life and
that they might have it more abundantly. I AM the Good
Shepherd. The Good Shepherd gives His life for the sheep.
But he that is a hireling and not the Shepherd whose own
sheep the sheep are not, sees the Wolf coming and leaves
the sheep and flees and the Wolf catches them and scat-
ters the sheep. The hired hand flees because he is a hired*

hand, and he does not care for the sheep. I AM the Good Shepherd and know My sheep and I AM known of Mine. As the Father knows Me, even so I know the Father. I lay down My life for the sheep. And other sheep I have which are not of this fold. Them also, I must bring, and they shall hear My voice and there shall be one-fold, and one Shepherd. Therefore, does my Father love Me because I lay down My life that I might take it again. No man takes it from Me, but I lay it down of Myself. I have power to lay it down and I have power to take it again. This commandment have I received of My Father." John 10:1-18.

"Remember therefore from where you have fallen, and repent, and do the 1st works, or else I will come to you quickly and remove your candle stick out of its place, except you repent. But this you have to your credit, you hate the deeds of the Nicolaitans, which I also hate. He that has an ear let him hear what the Spirit says into the churches. To him that overcomes will I give the right to eat of the tree of life which is in the middle of the paradise of God." Revelation 2:5-7

Jesus Is The Way.

Jesus Is The Good Shepard.

Jesus Is The Door.

Jesus Is The Truth.

Jesus Is The Life.

CHAPTER 5

TYPOLOGY

Hopefully at this point, you are beginning to see the "typology" contained in the Bible. (type / antitype).

As previously covered in Chapter 1, I would like to reiterate the definition of the Greek word TUPOS...

"a die (as struck), i.e. (by implication) a stamp or scar; by analogy, a shape, i.e., a statue, (figuratively) style or resemblance; specifically, a sampler ("type"), i.e., a model (for imitation) or instance (for warning)."

Just as a teacher in a classroom might present a picture rather than data to illustrate a difficult concept before teaching the concept directly, so does our Creator teach difficult concepts by painting a picture.

Sometimes we need to stand back and look at the picture in its entirety to grasp the concept. Kind of like the person in the forest who cannot see the forest for the trees... but when viewed from a hot air balloon the entirety of the forest becomes visible.

This is the difference between Micro-exegesis and Macro-exegesis, two theological terms which are different approaches to the study of scripture. While both have their merits, the "Macro" method (looking at the big picture from the hot air balloon) is the approach that you will need to employ to grasp some of the concepts that will be presented in this book.

Many things in the Old Testament such as: events, holy days, persons, tabernacle furnishings, etc. are valid as historically accurate in themselves, but also serve as an illustration, or "type" of what was to come.

Case in point:

The Rock giving water is a type of Christ's crucifixion and the pouring out of the Holy Spirit.

The Bread in the wilderness is a type of Christ who sustains us in our "wilderness" wanderings.

The Passover Lamb is a type of Christ atoning for the sins of humanity.

Adam is a type of Christ in that he affected the course of history singlehandedly by his disobedience and Jesus by his obedience...

"Wherefore, as by one man sin entered the world, and death by sin; and so, death passed upon all men, for all have sinned: (For until the law sin was in the world: but sin is not imputed when there is no law. Nevertheless, death reigned from Adam to Moses, even over them that had not sinned after the similitude of Adam's transgression, WHO IS THE FIGURE OF HIM THAT WAS TO COME. But not as the offence, so also is the free gift. For if through the offence of one many be dead, much more the grace of God and the gift by grace, which is by one man, Jesus Christ, has abounded unto many. And not as it was by one that sinned, so is the gift: for the judgment was by one to condemnation, but the free gift is of many offences unto justification. For if by one man's offence death reigned by one; much more they which receive abundance of grace and of the gift of righteousness shall reign in life by one, Jesus Christ). Therefore, as by the offence of one judgment came upon all men to condemnation; even so by

the righteousness of one the free gift came upon all men unto justification of life. For as by one man's disobedience many were made sinners, so by the obedience of one shall many be made righteous. Moreover, the law entered, that the offence might abound. But where sin abounded, grace did much more abound: That as sin has reigned unto death, even so might grace reign through righteousness unto eternal life by Jesus Christ our Lord." Romans 5:12-21

As you can see by this example; especially important theological concepts and truths are conveyed through type / antitype.

Symbolism, parables, shadows and allegory all play important roles in theological interpretation as well. Jesus employed all these methods and more in His teachings... So much so, that His closest friends did not understand what He was trying to convey a lot of the time.

"And the disciples came, and said to Him, "Why do you speak to them in parables?" He answered and said, "Because it is given unto you to know the MYSTERIES of the kingdom of heaven, but to them it is not given." Matthew 13:10-11

In other words, some will understand, and some will not.

"I will open My mouth in a parable: I will utter dark sayings of old." Psalm78:2

"All these things Jesus spoke unto the multitude in parables; and without a parable He spoke not unto them: That it might be fulfilled which was spoken by the

prophet, saying, "I will open My mouth in parables; I will utter things which have been kept secret from the foundation of the world." Matthew 13:34-35

Everyone loves a "secret," Right? A great "mystery" that is realized? Have you ever had that "AH-HA!" or "Eureka!" moment? Of course you have. It is like an epiphany... a moment of sudden revelation, or insight.

The word of God will come alive in these moments. I cannot tell you how many times I have experienced a special insight or revelation of a passage of scripture that I had read maybe 100 times before; but on the 101st time something just jumped off the page and I saw the passage in a whole new light, or frame of reference. It is extremely exciting to me.

Peter identifies the flood in the days of Noah as a "type" and baptism as the "antitypical" fulfillment.

"For it is better, if the will of God be so, that you suffer for well doing, than for evil doing. For Christ also has once suffered for sins, the just for the unjust, that he might bring us to God, being put to death in the flesh, but quickened by the Spirit: By which also He went and preached unto the spirits in prison; which sometimes were disobedient, when once the longsuffering of God waited in the days of Noah, while the Ark was being prepared, wherein few, that is, 8 souls were saved by water. The like FIGURE IS BAPTISM which does also now save us, not the putting away of the filth of the flesh, but the answer of a good conscience towards God, by the resurrection of Jesus Christ." 1 Peter 3:17-21.

Paul identifies the miraculous deliverance through the parting of the Red Sea as a "type" of baptism.

"Moreover brethren, I would not that you should be ignorant, how that all our fathers were under the cloud, and all passed through the sea; And were all baptized unto Moses in the cloud and in the sea." 1 Corinthians 10:1-2

Abraham was told by the LORD to take his son Isaac up to Mount Moriah and sacrifice him there. There are several typological occurrences contained in this story... The first, that it occurred on "the third day" (which puts it in the "midst of the week"); Just as Jesus was slain in the midst of the week.

"Then on the 3rd day Abraham lifted up his eyes and saw the place (M. Moriah) afar off." Genesis 22:4.

"And He shall confirm the covenant with many for one week: and IN THE MIDST OF THE WEEK, He shall cause the sacrifice and the oblation to cease..." Daniel 9:27.

He caused the animal sacrifices and the oblation to cease by fulfilling them on the cross. Jesus was crucified literally in the middle of the week (on Wednesday). His crucifixion was also in the middle of the final week of years (70th week of Daniel).

I know, and I am well aware, that those of you who have study bibles have commentary on Daniel 9:27 that probably speaks of the "Antichrist" and the commentary separates the final week of the 70-week prophecy and moves it into the end of this current dispensation. This is a grave error, and I will explain in the next chapter... but first, back to Abraham / Isaac...

The second is: Just as God provided a "substitute" sacrifice with the ram, He also provided a substitute sacrifice for every person who has ever lived... Jesus Christ, His only son.

Thirdly, just as the substitute sacrifice (ram) had briars wrapped around his horns and head which had him bound to the thicket, Jesus wore a "crown" of thorns around His head.

> *"And Abraham lifted up his eyes, and looked, and behind him was a ram caught in a thicket by his horns: and Abraham went and took the ram and offered him up for a burnt offering instead of his son." Genesis 22:13*

> *"And the soldiers platted a crown of thorns, (the sign of earth's curse {Genesis 3:17-18}) and put it on His head, and they put on Him a purple robe." John 19:2*

There are many, many more examples of typology contained in the Word of God, but I have hopefully shared enough occurrences with you so that you may see and understand concepts that I will present to you in subsequent chapters.

Jesus Is The Word.

CHAPTER 6

ESCHATOLOGY

There are 2 major fields of study of prophecy... especially eschatology. (The study of last things). The first being the FUTURIST view. The second being the HISTORICIST view. Within this framework, there are also other divisions: Amillennialism, Postmillennialism, Historic Premillennialism, and Dispensationalism... and within each of these there are even more divisions...

According to Futurism, the 70th week of Daniel will occur at some point in the future, culminating in seven years (or 3.5 years depending on denomination) of Tribulation and the appearance of the ANTICHRIST.

Such a thesis is paradigmatic for Dispensational Premillennialism. In contradistinction, Historic Premillennialism may or may not posit Daniel 70th week as future yet retain the thesis of the future fulfillment of many of the prophecies of Major and Minor prophets, the teachings of Christ (e.g., Matthew 24) and the Book of Revelation.

Dispensationalist Interpretation

Dispensationalists typically hold that a "hiatus", which some refer to as a "biblical parenthesis," occurred between the 69th and the 70th week of the prophecy, into which the "church age" is inserted (also known as the "gap theory" of Daniel nine). The 70th week of the prophecy is expected to commence after the rapture of the church, which will incorporate the establishment of an economic system using the number 666, the reign of the beast (the Antichrist), the false religious system (the harlot), the Great Tribulation and Armageddon.

Controversy exists regarding the antecedent of "he" in Daniel 9:27. Many within the ranks of premillennialism do not affirm the "confirmation of the covenant" is made by Jesus Christ (as do many Amillennarians) but the antecedent of "he" in verse 27 refers to verse 26 ("the prince who is to come"- i.e., the Antichrist). This view holds that Antichrist will make a "treaty" as the prince of the covenant (i.e., "the prince who is to come") with Israel's future leadership at the commencement of the 70th week of Daniel's prophecy; in the midst of the week, the Antichrist will break the treaty and commence persecution against a regathered Israel.

I Find This Interpretation To Be Erroneous.

All Protestant reformers used the day / year principle of prophetic interpretation. The commandment to restore and to build Jerusalem unto the Messiah the Prince (Daniel 9:25) was given by King Artaxerxes in 456. B.C. With that year as our starting point, 490 literal years (70 x 7) brings us to the autumn of 34 A.D. See Ezra 7:11- 26. Working back one prophetic week or seven literal years brings us to the baptism of Jesus in 27 A.D. in the midst, or the middle, of the last week of the prophecy, Jesus was cut off meaning crucified in 31 A.D.... So, this cannot be a future fulfillment of prophecy, but history. The full 490 years brings us to 34 A.D. when Steven was stoned, and persecution began. Because the 70 weeks are a sealed prophecy (see Daniel 9:24), no futurist is authorized to unseal it.

And, Daniel spoke of the "time of the end" saying this:

"But you O Daniel, shut up the words, and seal the book, UNTIL THE TIME OF THE END: many shall run to and fro, and KNOWLEDGE SHALL BE INCREASED." Daniel 12:4

How Fast Is Knowledge Increasing?

My research of what is called: "The Doubling Curve" says that up until the year 1900 knowledge doubled every 100 years. By 1945, the rate was every 25 years, and the rate today is every 12 months or every 12 hours... Depending on which statistics you read... the point is: WE ARE LIVING IN THE LAST DAYS!

Look at the other part of Daniel's end time scenario:

"Many Shall Run To And Fro."

Think about it, in 1804, Englishman Richard Trevithick launched the first practical steam locomotive which traveled a whooping 10 miles per hour. Before that, travel was limited to horseback, hot air balloon, ship, wagon or walking... All of which were terribly slow modes of transportation compared to today.

Imagine if you will, that you can see the earth from near space in the year 1700... there are no airplanes, no automobiles, trains, motorcycles, bullet trains, no rockets blasting off from the surface.

Now imagine the same scenario only now it is the year 2021. Airspace is congested with commercial airliners traveling just under the speed of sound, automobiles congesting every roadway at rush hour, etc.

It is like a fire ant mound... little movement until the mound is disturbed! But put your foot on the mound and watch what happens!

"Many shall run to and fro."

Now that we have established that we are in the "time of the end" and "knowledge is increasing" why would we buy-in to ancient doctrines of eschatology? We should not. Not if knowledge is increasing. (Which it is).

Polycarp (ca. 69 – 155) warned that everyone who preached false doctrine was an antichrist.

Irenaeus (2nd cen. A.D.) identified the Antichrist with Paul's Man of Sin, Daniel's Little Horn, and John's Beast of Revelation 13.

Tertullian (ca. 160 – 220 A.D.) held somewhat similar views as did: Hippolytus (ca. 170 – 236) and Origen (ca. 185 – 254).

These are commonly referred to as some of the "Church Father's." Church doctrine by necessity was laid down into dogma, creeds, Papal Bulls, and other writings which have been built and expounded upon for centuries... Which has brought us to the mess that we are in today. With so many different views of the end time which I have already mentioned, which view is the correct view? They cannot all be right!

It seems to me that it is a mess of CONFUSION! (Babylon).

Let us see if we can straighten out some of the confusion, starting with THE ANTICHRIST.

CHAPTER 7

THE ANTICHRIST

In the last chapter, we learned that mainstream Christian theologians have been building upon dogma handed down from the early Church "fathers." I believe this to be a mistake because the Bible will explain itself if one lets it... along with the help of the Holy Spirit who will lead us into all truth.

> In other words, why would I let some guy who lived
> 19 centuries ago tell me what I should believe about
> the "end times?" Times that I am living through!

Another problem that I have with mainstream Christian doctrine is this: many denominations say that the "canon" of scripture (66 books) has been "closed." The Easter letter of Athanasius (A.D.367) was the first to list the 66 books which comprise the "canon" that we know today as the Bible. These 66 books were upheld at the synods of Hippo (A.D. 393) and Carthage (A.D. 397) as the authoritative Word of God and all other ancient writings are to be excluded.

> I strongly disagree. Again, why would I let a bunch of
> guys who lived 1600 years ago tell me what I can
> or cannot read on my quest to grow closer to God?
> Why would I?

I read most every ancient writing that I can get my hands on and let that still, small voice tell me if I should read it and believe it or not, isn't that one of the functions of the Holy Spirit?

In fact, our Bible speaks of other writings, which are not included in the canon, in an authoritative manner at: 2Samuel 1:18, Joshua 10:13, and 2 Chronicles 9:29 just to name a few. So, let us see if we can let the bible explain itself, and not enter our study with erroneous pre-conceived notions.

> In other words, forget what you have been taught by men and let the Word of God and the Holy Spirit teach you.

The word: ANTICHRIST only appears in the Scriptures 5 times. What a great place to start, to understand what or who the "antichrist" is...

> *"Little children, it is the last time: and as you have heard that ANTICHRIST shall come, even now are there many ANTICHRISTS; whereby we know that it is the last time."* 1 John 2:18

The apostle writes that in the first century people were told that ANTICHRIST would come, and then says that EVEN NOW (the 1st century A.D.) are there MANY ANTICHRISTS. He did not say that we should look for THE ANTICHRIST in the end of the age. NO! He said that there were already MANY ANTICHRISTS. This one verse contains the first 2 occurrences of the word ANTICHRIST.

Let us move on to the 3rd occurrence.

> *"Who is a liar but he that denies that Jesus is the Christ? He is ANTICHRIST, that denies the Father and the Son. Whosoever denies the Son, the same has not the Father: [but] he that acknowledges the Son has the Father also."* 1 John 2:22-23.

Anyone, who denies the divinity or Sonship of Jesus is ANTI-CHRIST... I think John just gave us the definition and pre-re-quisites of ANTICHRIST. Also, John says (and I am paraphrasing) that a person cannot say that Jesus was just a prophet and still have a relationship with the Father because to deny the Son is to deny the Father as well. Remember this 3rd occurrence of ANTI-CHRIST and read it several times because we will revisit it later.

Let us move on to the 4th occurrence of ANTICHRIST.

> *"Beloved, believe not every spirit, but try the spirits whether they are of God, because many false prophets are gone out into the world. Hereby you know the Spirit of God; every spirit that confesses that Jesus Christ has come in the flesh is of God; and every spirit that confesses not that Jesus Christ has come in the flesh is not of God; and this is that spirit of ANTICHRIST, whereof you have heard that it should come, and even now already it is in the world." 1 John 4:1-3.*

John says it again, You guys have heard that the ANTICHRIST would come and guess what? He is ALREADY HERE! And here is a way that you can identify - "THE ANTICHRIST"- ANYONE, and I say again, ANYONE who denies the divinity of Jesus (that He is God) or denies that He is the SON OF GOD, is ANTICHRIST.... And remember, there are a lot of them already here so do not let anyone deceive you into thinking that the ANTICHRIST is something or someone who will appear in the future!

He's ALREADY HERE!

I am very much paraphrasing, but that is what he was saying. Let us move on to the final occurrence of the word ANTICHRIST.

> *"For many deceivers are entered into the world who confess not that Jesus Christ (God) has come in the flesh. This*

is a deceiver and an ANTICHRIST." 2 John 7.

Any time that God wants to get our attention He will put something in scripture more than once.

Wake Up! He Is Saying.

All 5 occurrences of the word ANTICHRIST deal with 2 or more of these main points:

#1. You have heard that the ANTICHRIST would come.

#2. He is already here.

#3. There are MANY of them.

#4. They deny the divinity and Sonship of Jesus.

#5. By denying the Son, they have denied the Father.

So now the questions arise:

#1. If the ANTICHRISTS are many and have been here since the 1st century, who are they?

#2. If waiting for the ANTICHRIST to appear on the world stage in the future is false doctrine, then what about the "Man of Sin" that Paul spoke of? Who is He?

#3. Who is the "Prince that shall come" of Daniel 9:26?

The first question to answer is #1. Who are they? (ANTICHRISTS).

ISLAM

Muslims admit that Jesus was a prophet and that He did many mighty works... But they deny that He was the Son of God (Allah) or that He was God.

Islam's Holy Book, the Koran, does not have "chapters" as the

Christian Bible does, but is divided by "Surahs..." Below is an excerpt from the Koran, Written by the "Prophet" Muhammad.

Surah 18

AL-KAHF
(THE CAVE)

1. All the praises and thanks are to Allah Who has sent down to His slave (Muhammad) the Book (Quran) and has not placed therein any crookedness.
2. (He has made it) straight to give warning (to the disbelievers) of a severe punishment from Him, and to give glad tidings to the believers (in the Oneness of Allah – Islamic Monotheism) who do righteous deeds, that they shall have a fair reward (i.e., paradise).
3. They shall abide therein forever.
4. And to warn those (Jews, Christians, and pagans) who say, "Allah (God) has begotten a Son."
5. No knowledge have they of such a thing, nor had their fathers. Mighty is the word that comes out of their mouths... THEY UTTER NOTHING BUT A LIE.

Well, I guess I just pissed off every Muslim on the planet! Oooo-oooppsss! Hey, John the apostle said that if you deny that Jesus is the Son of God YOU ARE ANTICHRIST!!!

JUDAISM

The theological beliefs of Judaism on the coming of a Messiah have not been altered since the time of Jesus. Judaism believes that the Temple must be rebuilt and that the "true" Messiah will come in the power and glory of an earthly ruler and squash any opposition to the nation of Israel.

Judaism, like Islam, is monotheistic and thus denies the Trinity. They, like Islam, believe that Yahweh has not begotten a Son.

The Jews and chief priests brought accusation against Jesus before Pontus Pilate and called for His Crucifixion,

> *"When the chief priests therefore and officers saw Him, they cried out, saying, "Crucify him, crucify him," Pilate said, "You take him and crucify him: for I find no fault in him." The Jews answered him, "We have a law, and by our law he ought to die, BECAUSE HE MADE HIMSELF THE SON OF GOD." John 19:6-7.*

Like Islam, Judaism also DENIES THAT JESUS IS THE SON OF GOD. Therefore, according to the Word of God, all Judaism is ANTICHRIST.

I am asking you, the reader of this book, to use your own brain for a moment and do not look to the commentary in your own bible to see what some so-called "biblical scholar" wants you to believe…. OKAY?

If there were "MANY ANTICHRISTS" already in the world in the 1st century when John wrote his epistles, why do most people think that an "ANTICHRIST" figure, or person has yet to rear His ugly head on the world stage? It certainly does not make any sense. But I will answer the question for you, but please, please, do not take my word for it, do your own research and ask the Holy Spirit to reveal the truth to you.

The reason is:

1. Most people like "Study Bibles" so that when they come to a difficult passage of scripture, they can look down in the commentary for clarification… not realizing that the commentary is written by a fallible human

being who may be deceived and passing on false doctrine... remember, John warned of false prophets. A much better approach would be to use a bible which does not have commentary and get a good concordance and lexicon and to ask the Holy Spirit to lead you into the truth... just remember that the Lexicons and Concordances are written by fallible human beings as well. Use your own common sense and listen to that "still, small voice."

2. The Bible itself tells us how to study it and people (theologians who write commentary included) don't tend to follow the formula, "Whom shall He teach knowledge? And whom shall He make to understand DOCTRINE? Them that are weaned from the milk and drawn from the breasts. For precept must be upon precept, precept upon precept, line upon line, line upon line; here a little, and there a little." Isaiah 28:9-10. In other words, the entirety of scripture must be HARMONIZED. But so-called "Biblical Scholars" sometimes do not do that. The tendency is to take a difficult passage and instead of letting the Bible explain itself, line upon line, here a little and there a little, they cast the difficulty into the future and use one or two other passages to back up their theory. Or they just go along with the status quo. I will speak more about this in #4.

3. People are sheep, plain and simple. Like sheep, people tend to go the way of the crowd. The adversary does not need to deceive the whole world individually, NO! All he needs to do is get a few going the wrong way and the rest will follow. "And the great dragon was cast out, that old serpent, called the Devil and Satan, WHICH DECEIVES THE WHOLE WORLD: he was cast out into the earth, and his angels were cast out with him." Revelation 12:9. "For such are false apostles, deceitful workers, transforming themselves into the apostles of Christ. And no marvel: for Satan himself is trans-

formed into an angel of light. Therefore, it is no great thing if his ministers also be transformed as the ministers of righteousness; whose end shall be according to their works." 2Corinthians 11:13-15.

4. "Theologians" don't want to upset the "status quo." It is much easier to go along with what has been handed down to us through the centuries masquerading as "true church doctrine." I will give you an example, and believe me there are many to choose from, but here is one example of false doctrine handed down to us from antiquity: Friday Crucifixion and Sunday resurrection. Jesus was not crucified on a Friday and most so-called "theologians" know this to be true but find it easier to "not rock the boat," and to "not make waves" upon the stage of biblical "truth." I will prove to you in the next chapter that it is false doctrine.

These are just a few of the reasons why people are blind to the reality that there are BILLIONS of ANTICHRISTS in our world today... there are more reasons, but that is not the scope of this book and I believe that I have given you sufficient evidence to at least get you to start seeing the truth.

If I were the Devil, I would want everyone on the planet to think that the Temple must be rebuilt, and an "ANTICHRIST" person must sit in that temple and pretend that he is God before Jesus can return! (Which are what millions of Christians have been led to believe).

WHY? Because if Christians think that Jesus is not coming until this happens, then they would not see the time approaching and will be caught unaware.

Believe me when I say: THE PHYSICAL TEMPLE WILL NOT BE REBUILT IN JERUSALEM... PERIOD. The Dome of the Rock, an Islamic shrine, stands on the Temple Mount. It is the 3rd most holy site in all of Islam. Think about it. Use common sense.

Paul says that believers are the Temple now with Christ as the Chief Cornerstone. We will cover the Temple in a later chapter.

In summary: the doctrine of an ANTICHRIST figure coming on the world scene, just before the "Rapture" or 2nd Coming of Jesus, has been handed down to us through the (almost 2) millennia since Christ's crucifixion; by the church.

Clement of Rome, Ignatius of Antioch, Polycarp of Smyrna, Papias of Hierapolis, Justin Martyr, Irenaeus of Lyons, Clement of Alexandria, Origen of Alexandria and more, are considered to be the "Church Fathers" of the Christian faith. In traditional dogmatic theology, authors considered to be "Church Fathers" are treated as authoritative.

But once again I will pose the question, If Daniel says that in the "time of the end, knowledge shall increase," then WHY would I treat something that someone wrote hundreds of years ago as "authoritative" and ignore the teachings found in the bible? In other words: Church doctrine has been that ANTICHRIST will appear one day in the future.... BUT IN THESE LAST DAYS I'M TELLING YOU THAT THERE ARE BILLIONS OF ANTICHRISTS ALL AROUND US... In the Mosque's, in the Synagogue's, in the convenience stores, in the motel's, in the banks, at the supermarkets, they are everywhere! And yes, even in Christian Churches.

Jesus Is The Son Of God.

CHAPTER 8

THE CRUCIFIXION

F alse doctrine is passed down from generation to generation. The Friday Crucifixion of Jesus is just one of many examples. "Good Friday" has been celebrated in commemoration of the Crucifixion of Jesus since antiquity. But was He really crucified on a Friday? No, He was not. He was Crucified on a Wednesday, on the Passover, year 31 A.D.

The Sign Of The Times

"The Pharisees also with the Sadducees came and asked Him to show them a sign from heaven. He (Jesus) answered and said to them, "When it is evening, you say, it will be fair weather; for the sky is red. And in the morning, it will be foul weather today; for the sky is red and lowering. O you hypocrites, you can discern the face of the sky; but you cannot discern the signs of the times? A wicked and adulterous generation seeks after a sign; and there shall no sign be given unto it except the sign of the prophet Jonah." Matthew 16:1-4.

I am asking you, brethren, can you discern the signs of the times? I hope so. Jesus has given us ample evidence in His Word to be able to discern the "signs of the times" that we live in.

> *"Then certain of the scribes and of the Pharisees an-*
> *swered, saying, "Master, we would like to see a sign from*
> *you." But He answered and said unto them, "An evil and*
> *adulterous generation seeks after a sign; and there shall*
> *no sign be given to it, but the sign of the prophet Jonah:*
> *For as Jonah was THREE DAYS and THREE NIGHTS in the*
> *whale's belly; so shall the Son of Man be THREE DAYS and*
> *THREE NIGHTS in the heart of the earth." (The tomb).*
> *Matthew 12:38-40.*

A Friday crucifixion only accounts for 2 nights in the tomb... Friday night and Saturday night.

A Friday crucifixion only accounts for 1 day in the tomb... Saturday.

> Was Jesus a liar and messed up the ONLY SIGN given
> to that generation? I think not!!!

The erroneous observance of "Good Friday" has been passed down through the ages and when "theologians" (I use that term loosely) are confronted with the passages in Matthew which clearly state 3 Days and 3 Nights, they are forced into making up all manner of nonsense to justify their position, such as: "The 3 days and 3 Nights are not literal days and nights... in ancient times any part of a day was considered a full day so Friday, Saturday and Sunday is what Jesus meant."

HOGWASH! BOLONEY! ARE YOU SERIOUS! HA! YOU'VE GOT TO BE KIDDING!!??!!?

While it may be true that according to Hebrew idiom "3 days" could be interpreted to mean any part of 3 days and not necessarily 3 – 24-hour days, when Jesus added "3 nights" the use of the idiom goes out the window.

Three days and three nights becomes exactly that... 3 full days and 3 full nights.

No, Jesus is not a liar and once again, the Bible will explain itself if you let it.

The confusion arises because Jesus was plainly Crucified on the Preparation Day which many believe to be the Preparation Day to the Weekly Sabbath, which occurs every 7 days. Saturday being the Sabbath and Friday the Preparation. All the cooking, cleaning, chores, etc. were to be done on Friday (preparation) so they could rest on the Sabbath (sundown Friday to sundown Saturday).

The trouble is: JESUS WASN'T CRUCIFIED ON THE PREPARATION TO THE WEEKLY SABBATH, HE WAS CRUCIFIED ON THE PASSOVER WHICH IS THE PREPARATION DAY TO THE FIRST "HIGH DAY" SABBATH OF THE FEAST OF UNLEAVENED BREAD. TWO SABBATHS, TWO PREPARATION DAYS!

Here is the one verse in the Bible that tells us He was not crucified on the Preparation Day to the weekly Sabbath, but on the Preparation Day of the High Day Sabbath (the 15th of Abib or Nissan).

> "The Jews, therefore, because it was the preparation that the bodies should not remain upon the cross on the sabbath day (for that sabbath day WAS A HIGH DAY) besought Pilate that their legs might be broken, and that they might be taken away." John 19:31

Jesus had just died. It is written that anyone who hangs on a tree at night is cursed. Sundown was rapidly approaching. The Jews wanted Pilate to order that the legs be broken to expedite death so the bodies could be taken down and put in the tombs before sundown. Pilate agreed and when the soldiers came to break their legs, they saw that Jesus had already expired so they did not break His legs but did thrust a spear into His side.

"And if a man has committed a sin worthy of death and he is to be put to death and you hang him on a tree: His body shall not remain all night upon the tree, but you shall bury him that day; (for he that is hanged is accursed of God)." Deuteronomy 21:22-23

"And the LORD spoke to Moses, saying, "Speak to the children of Israel, and say to them concerning the feasts of the LORD, which you shall proclaim to be holy convocations, even these are my feasts. Six days must work be done but the 7th day is the Sabbath, a holy convocation; you shall do no work there in; it is the Sabbath of the Lord in all your dwellings. These are the feast of the Lord, even holy convocation's, which you shall proclaim in their seasons. In the 14th day of the first month at evening is the Lord's Passover. And on the 15th day of the same month is the feast of unleavened bread unto the Lord; seven days you must eat unleavened bread. The first day you shall have a holy convocation; You shall do no servile work therein. (Making the 15th day of the 1st month the first 'high day' sabbath of the year)." Leviticus 23:1-7.

Jesus was crucified on the Passover, which is ALWAYS the Preparation Day (14th day of the 1st month) to the first "High Day" Sabbath (15th day of the 1st month) of the Feast of Unleavened Bread.

Before I give you the timeline of the 3 days and 3 nights, we need to examine just what a "day" and "night" are in Gods eyes...

"And God called the light Day and the darkness He called Night. And the evening (dark) and the morning (light) were the first day."

"And God called the firmament Heaven. And the evening and the morning were the second day."

"And the evening and the morning were the third day."

"And the evening and the morning were the fourth day."

"And the evening and the morning were the fifth day."

"And God saw everything that He had made, and behold, it was very good. And the evening and the morning were the sixth day."

"And on the seventh day God ended His work which He had made; and He rested on the Seventh Day from all His work which He had made. And God blessed the seventh day and sanctified it: because He had rested from all His work which God created and made." Genesis 1:5,8,13,19,23,31. 2:2-3.

It makes absolutely no sense to divide our days at 12 o'clock MIDNIGHT. There is no natural divide there.

It also makes absolutely no sense to divide our years in the dead of winter, on January 1st, there is no natural divide there either.

As you can see from the passages in Genesis 1 and 2, God divides His days at Sundown. And you will also notice that the night portion (evening) is the first part of the day, not the ending of the day.

God also divides His Years in the springtime, when trees are budding and coming back to life, the grass is green and growing again... etc.

It makes much more sense to go by God's calendar where there are natural divisions instead of man's way of doing things where there is no natural division.

> So, keep in mind that sundown to sundown constitutes 1 day.

Another fact you need to be aware of is that by the time of Jesus, the "Passover" came to mean the entire 8 - day observance of the Passover and the 7 days of the Feast of Unleavened Bread. It was not so in the wilderness wanderings of Israel but over time "Passover" became synonymous with the entire observance... from the 14th of Nissan (Nissan or Abib, either is correct) to the last day of the Feast of Unleavened Bread on the 21st day of Nissan.

Another fact that you need to know is that when it says in scripture "about the 6th hour" or, "about the 3rd hour" it is not talking about 6 o'clock or 3 o'clock. It is the 6th hour from sunup or sundown. To simplify this process, the practice of the day was to recon time from 6am or 6pm.

Therefore, the 6th hour refers to either noon (6 + 6 = 12) or midnight. And the 3rd hour refers to either 9am or 9pm.

> I know it is a lot to receive, but to understand how God sees time is crucial to understanding many passages of scripture. With this in mind, here is the timeline of

Christ's Last Day:

Sundown, on Tuesday, marked the beginning of the Passover, Abib (or Nissan) 14th. Jesus observed the Passover with His disciples in the "upper room" on this Tuesday evening,

> *"Now the first day of the Feast of Unleavened Bread (Passover) the disciples came to Jesus, saying to Him, "Where shall we prepare for you to eat the Passover?" And He said, "Go into the city to such a man and say to him, "The Master says, My time is at hand; I will keep the Passover at your house with my disciples." And the disciples did as Jesus had appointed them; and they made ready the Passover. Now when even (sundown) was come, He sat down with the twelve." Matthew 26:17-20*

This is the night or evening, that Jesus instituted a new observance of partaking the Bread and Wine which we call "communion."

Immediately after this "Last Supper" with His disciples, Judas Iscariot left to betray Him.

> *"He then having received the sop went immediately out: and it was night." (Tuesday night before midnight).*

Jesus and His disciples then went to the Garden of Gethsemane and Jesus prayed. While at Gethsemane, Judas Iscariot returned to Jesus with soldiers and Jesus was arrested. They led Him to Annas first, then Caiaphas, Pilate, Herod, and back to Pilate... the trials continued throughout the night. Matthew 26:57 – 27:31, Mark 14:53 – 15:20, Luke 22:54 – 23:25, John 18:12 - 19:16.

> *"And it was the Preparation of the Passover, and about the sixth hour (midnight Tuesday night); and he (Pilate) said to the Jews, "Behold your King!" But they cried out,*

"Away with Him, crucify Him." Pilate said to them, "Shall I crucify your King?" The chief priests answered, "We have no king but Caesar." Then he delivered Him unto them to be crucified. And they took Jesus and led Him away." John 19:14-16.

Jesus was then nailed to the Cross Wednesday morning about 9am.

"And it was the 3rd hour (9am Wednesday morning) and they crucified Him." Mark 15:25.

Then from 12 o'clock noon on Wednesday until 3 o'clock in the afternoon it was dark.

"Now from the sixth hour (Noon) there was darkness over all the land until the ninth hour (3pm)." Matthew 27:45, Mark 15:33, Luke 23:44.

Shortly after 3pm on Wednesday afternoon, on the 14th day of Abib, Jesus died. Matthew 27:50, Mark 15:37, Luke 23:46, John 19:30.

Jesus was buried in haste before sunset. (Our Wednesday about 6pm).

"When the evening was come, there came a rich man of Arimathea, named Joseph, who also himself was Jesus' disciple: He went to Pilate, and begged him for the body of Jesus. Then Pilate commanded the body to be delivered. And when Joseph had taken the body, he wrapped it in a clean linen cloth and laid it in his own new tomb, which he had hewn out in the rock: and he rolled a great stone to the door of the sepulchre and departed." Matthew

27:57-60.

So, Jesus was put in the tomb, on the Passover, just before sundown, on Wednesday, Abib 14, 31 A.D.

As soon as the sun set, the 1st day of the Feast of Unleavened Bread began. Sundown marked the beginning of the "High Day" Sabbath.

> *"The Jews, therefore, because it was the Preparation; that the bodies should not remain upon the cross on the Sabbath Day (FOR THAT SABBATH DAY WAS A HIGH DAY) ...John 19:31.*

To fulfill the "Sign of the Prophet Jonah" Jesus was in the tomb, Wednesday Night, Thursday Night, and Friday Night to fulfill the "3 nights," half of the "sign" given to that generation.

To fulfill the other half of the "sign" Jesus was in the tomb, Thursday (daylight hours}, Friday (daylight hours), and Saturday (daylight hours) fulfilling the "3 days."

Jesus was in the tomb 3 days and 3 nights, just like He said He would be. Matthew 12:40.

Tradition holds that Jesus was risen or resurrected, on Sunday morning and in a certain sense this is true if we remember that that day, (the 1st day of the week) began at sundown on Saturday night. Remember, God divides His days at sundown. All 4 gospels record that it was very early in the morning of the 1st day of the week that Mary Magdalene, Mary, and Salome came to the tomb and Jesus was already risen.

The book of John says that it was still dark. John 20:1.

So, there you have true doctrine. Wednesday was the Preparation Day to Thursday, a High Day Sabbath, and Friday was the Preparation Day to Saturday, the weekly Sabbath. Two Preparation Days and Two Sabbath Days.

Let the Bible explain itself. Harmonize the Scriptures. Do not use a study bible which will lead you astray in the commentary. Remember this:

A Pair Of Lips Can Say Anything.

Do not let a group of guys who lived 1600 or more years ago determine what you should accept as "doctrine." Remember the formula contained in the scriptures... Isaiah 28:9-10.

Remember also, that in the time of the end knowledge will increase.

Jesus Is Not A Liar.

Jesus Is The Antitypical Fulfillment Of Jonah In The Belly Of The Great Fish.

Jesus Is Risen.

CHAPTER 9

THE TEMPLE

Doing my research in preparation for this chapter, I wanted to know where this notion came from that there must be a 3rd Temple built again in Israel on the Temple Mount. (Where the Dome of the Rock stands today). I know how "theologians" twist the meaning of Daniel 9 and 2 Thessalonians 2:3-4 and I'm prepared to answer those misinterpretations, but thought that I may have overlooked something, so I googled "reasons people think the temple has to be rebuilt in Jerusalem…"

OH, MY GOODNESS! I watched 2 short videos from the Temple Institute: an organization that says that they cannot perform 202 of the 613 commandments contained in the Torah unless there is a Temple in Jerusalem to perform them at! They also said that preparations are being made now to raise a "red heifer" (see Numbers 19:2-9) to make the purification water. (Holy water) They also said that they have already constructed and made many of the vessels to furnish the Temple, including the Menorah.

RRRRRRRRRRRRRRRRRRINGGG

RRRRRRRRRRRIIINNNGGG, WAKE UP PEOPLE! (that is the alarm clock going off)

Are we listening to what the Jews have to say about prophecy now? Don't you remember? God closed their eyes, and plugged up their ears? (Isaiah 6:9-10) Remember? They are the ones who called for the crucifixion of Jesus! They want to build the Temple and start sacrificing animals again!

Hogwash! I say.

Let us address the main scriptures that Christian "theologians" (I still use that term loosely) use to back up their 3rd temple scenario.

Let us start with the 70-week prophecy of Daniel 9 using the 1 day = 1 literal year formula derived from Numbers 14:34 and Ezekiel 4:6. Most "theologians" agree that this is the formula that pertains to Daniel 9, and I agree as well.

> *"Seventy weeks are determined upon your people and upon your holy city, to finish the transgression, and to make an end of sins, and to make reconciliation for iniquity and to bring in everlasting righteousness, and to seal up the vision and prophecy and to anoint the most Holy." Daniel 9:24.*

We will break the passage up into small sections to understand the main points… and remember, do not take my word for what it means, do your own investigation and listen to that still small voice.

"Seventy weeks" 70 X 7 = 490, refers to 490 literal years.

"Determined" comes from the Hebrew word: CHATHAK and means, to cut off.

So, what is this 490-year period "cut off" from? Answer: The 2300-day (literal 2300 years) prophecy of Daniel 8:14.

And who or what does the 490-year prophecy concern? Answer: Your people, (Israel) and your Holy City. (Jerusalem).

Why? Answer: to finish the transgression. God is merciful to His chosen people, and He raises up Prophets to take a message of repentance to them repeatedly, but human beings in general, and

Israel specifically, are a "stiff necked" people.

> We do not like being told what to do even if it is for our
> own good.

But God gives us time to repent and turn back to Him because He is merciful and longsuffering... But He is also the Righteous Judge, and it is this judgement that will come if Israel does not repent in the time allotted. In this case, the time allotted is 490 years. Look at it as a time of "PROBATION." Probation for the chosen people and the city.

A similar time of "probation" concerning the prophet Jeremiah comes to mind. God told Jeremiah to warn His people,

> *"The LORD has sent unto you all his servants the prophets, rising early in sending them; but you have not listened, nor inclined your ear to hear. They said turn again now everyone from his evil way, and from the evil of your doings, and dwell in the land that the LORD has given to you and to your father's forever and ever. And go not after other gods to serve them, and to worship them, and provoke Me not to anger with the works of your hands; and I will do you no hurt. Yet you have not listened unto Me, says the LORD; that you might provoke Me to anger with the works of your hands to your own hurt. Therefore, thus says the LORD of hosts; because you have not heard My words, I will send and take all the families of the north, says the LORD, and Nebuchadnez-zar the king of Babylon, My servant, and I will bring them against this land and against the inhabitants thereof and against all these nations round about, and will utterly destroy them, and make them an astonishment, and a hissing, and perpetual desolations. Moreover, I will take from them the voice of mirth, and the voice of gladness, the voice of the bridegroom, and the voice of the bride, the*

sound of the millstones, and the light of the candle. And this whole land shall be a desolation, and an astonishment; And these nations shall serve the king of Babylon 70 years." Jeremiah 25:4-11.

God was merciful, He gave them time to repent but they did not. The 490-year prophecy deals with basically the same scenario...

God is saying:

"You have 490 years to repent until My patience (longsuffering) runs out and I send the Gospel message to the Gentiles; send the sword upon you to scatter you (disperse) and DESOLATE the Holy City including the TEMPLE.

Let us continue:

"to make an end of sins and to make reconciliation for iniquity,"

Jesus took upon Himself "the sins of the world" while hanging on the cross, (that is why it was dark from noon until 3pm) and provided "reconciliation" for us, (i.e., atonement). No longer would there be a separation between us and God. (This was symbolized by the veil in the Temple tearing in two when Jesus gave up His Spirit and died on the cross). (Matthew 27:51).

"And to bring in everlasting righteousness,"

Since the death and resurrection of Jesus and the subsequent pouring out of the Holy Spirit at Pentecost, we have been in what is called "the Church Age," Jesus said this:

"The kingdom of God doesn't come with observation, neither shall they say, "Here it is! Or there it is! For behold,

the Kingdom of God is within you." Luke 17:20b,21.

"And to seal up the vision and prophecy, and to anoint the most Holy."

Some visions and prophecies are "sealed," some are not. The reason is apparent if you think about it: People are not supposed to understand until the vision or prophecy is "unsealed." In this case the "seal" is to be broken in the "time of the end,"

"But you, O Daniel, shut up the words, and SEAL THE BOOK, to the time of the end: many shall run to and fro and knowledge shall be increased." Daniel 12:4.

"And to anoint the most Holy."

Some study bibles will say in the commentary that this phrase "most Holy," never refers to a person... I strongly disagree... Jesus was "anointed" with the Holy Spirit which descended upon Him in the form of a dove at His baptism in the Jordan by His cousin John the Baptist. (John 1:32) And when He went into the Temple to start His earthly ministry, He quoted Isaiah 61:1-2a.

"The Spirit of the LORD is upon Me, because HE HAS ANOINTED ME to preach the gospel to the poor; He has sent me to heal the brokenhearted, to preach deliverance to the captives, and recovering of sight to the blind, to set at liberty them that are bruised, to preach the acceptable year of the Lord." Luke 4:18-19.

More evidence for Jesus to be the "anointed" one is found in Acts

4... Verses 25 and 26 are quoted from Psalm 2:1-2...

> *"Why do the heathen rage, and the people imagine a vain thing? The kings of the earth set themselves and the rulers take counsel together against the LORD and against HIS ANOINTED." Psalm 2:1-2.*

In Acts, it quotes the last part of the same passage but changes "His anointed" to "His Christ" leaving absolutely no doubt that Jesus is HIS ANOINTED.

> *"The kings of the earth stood up, and the rulers were gathered together against the LORD and against His Christ." Acts 4:26.*

The Hebrew Title, Mashiach, (Messiah) means: ANOINTED.

The Greek Title, Christos, (Christ) means: ANOINTED.

End of discussion let us move on.

> *"Know therefore and understand, that from the going forth of the commandment to restore and to build Jerusalem unto the Messiah the Prince shall be seven weeks, and threescore (60) and two weeks: the street shall be built again, and the wall, even in troublous times." Daniel 9:25*

This passage of scripture is particularly important for it gives us the starting point not only for the 490-year prophecy, but also the starting point for the prophecy that it is "cut out of..." the 2300-year prophecy of Daniel 8:14. The commandment to restore and to build Jerusalem is one of 2 decrees. The first can be found in Ezra 1:1-4 written by Cyrus, king of Persia in the 1st year of his reign, and the second in Ezra 7:11-26 written by Artaxerxes. The chronology must be reckoned, or counted, from the decree of Artaxerxes which was in 456 BCE. Notice that the 70 week or 490-year prophecy is broken up into 3 periods... a 7-week (49 year} period, a 62-week (434 year) period, and a final 1-week (7 year) period. The first 49-year period (7 weeks) represents the time it took to build the temple, from the decree to its completion. Building was halted for a time and then resumed after Artaxerxes' decree... this explains John 2:20

> *"then said the Jews, "Forty and six years was this temple in building, and will you rear it up in 3 days."*

Apparently, the time it took to gather the necessary materials for building, and for travel, and for the hiatus added up to 3 years... 46 + 3 = 49, (7 X 7 or 7 weeks). The second period of time is the 62 weeks. A "score" equals 20 years therefore, "threescore" equals 60 and 2 is 62. This time period extends from the completion of the Temple to the baptism of Jesus in the Jordan river by John the Baptist. Here is the math of the timeline: 456 BCE is the starting point. 456 – 49 = 407 (completion of the Temple). 407 BCE minus 434 (62X7) equals 27 AD (baptism of Jesus). Jesus began His ministry in the fall of 27 AD. This completes 69 weeks of the 70-week prophecy, leaving a final week (7 years) that we will cover shortly.

> *"The street shall be built again, and the wall, even in troublous times."*

The book of Nehemiah chronicles the building of the wall and reports that the peoples all around Jerusalem threatened the work of rebuilding so severely that,

> *"They which builded on the wall, and they that bare burdens, with those that laded, everyone with one of his hands wrought in the work, and with the other hand,*

held a weapon. For the builders, everyone had his sword girded by his side, and so builded. And he that sounded the trumpet was by me." Nehemiah 4:17-18.

Sounds Like Troublous Times To Me.

"And after threescore and two weeks (62X7=434) shall Messiah be cut off, but not for Himself: and the people of the prince that shall come shall destroy the city (Jerusalem) and the sanctuary (Temple); and the end thereof shall be with a flood, and unto the end of the war desolations are determined." Daniel 9:26.

Notice the word "after" is the Hebrew word ACHAR and is used in a wide variety of applications but means here: "after that" or "following after," This is important in the fact that one time period has ended, and another has begun. In other words, it says "after" threescore and two weeks because there is still 3 ½ years remaining of Jesus' earthly ministry before He is "cut off", (crucified).

The phrase

"but not for Himself"

is self-explanatory. He gave His life as a ransom for all of mankind.

"And the people of the prince that shall come shall destroy the city and the sanctuary"

refers to the siege of Jerusalem and subsequent destruction of the city and Temple by the Roman army led by Titus in 70 AD.

"And the end thereof shall be with a flood, and unto the end of the war desolations are determined."

After the city and the Temple were sacked in 70 AD, there was still opposition to the occupying Roman forces and the Zealots and other Jewish holdouts made their last stand at Masada, an ancient fortification on a hilltop overlooking the Dead Sea. The fort was under siege for 4 – 7 months.

According to Josephus, 960 men, women, and children perished at Masada... many had committed suicide. This ended the war in 73 AD.

"And He shall confirm the covenant with many for one week: and in the Midst of the week, He shall cause the sacrifice and the oblation to cease, and for the overspreading of abominations He shall make it desolate, even until the consummation and that determined shall be poured upon the desolate." Daniel 9:27.

Let Us Break It Down:

"And He shall confirm the covenant with many for one week."

From Jesus' baptism in the Jordan until the stoning of Stephen (Acts 7) there are 7 years. For the first 3 ½ years Jesus trained His disciples for ministry and then was crucified. For the next 3 ½ years His Disciples took the "covenant" (new covenant/gospel message) to Israel. It is only after the stoning of Stephen in 34

AD that the 490 years of the "70-week" prophecy expired.

This is why Jesus told His disciples to go unto the "lost sheep of Israel" exclusively.

> *"These twelve Jesus sent forth and commanded them saying, "Go not into the way of the Gentiles, and into any city of the Samaritans enter you not: But go rather to the lost sheep of the house of Israel. "Matthew 10:5-6.*

A Canaanite woman came to Jesus and wanted Him to help her daughter who was vexed with a devil... Jesus ultimately helps the woman but before He is persuaded, He told the woman,

> *"I am not sent but unto the lost sheep of the house of Israel." Matthew 15:24*

Why did He tell her no at first?

Answer: Because Probation for the Jews had not expired yet. The 490 years still had 4 or so years left. After the death and resurrection of Jesus, there were still 3 ½ years left... that's why Paul said,

> *"For I am not ashamed of the gospel of Christ: for it is the power of God unto salvation to everyone that believes; TO THE JEW FIRST, and also to the Greek." Romans 1:16.*

It's why Luke records:

> *"You are the children of the prophets, and of the covenant which God made with our fathers, saying unto Abraham, and in your seed shall all the kindreds of the earth be blessed. UNTO YOU FIRST God, having raised up His Son Jesus, SENT HIM TO BLESS YOU, in turning away every*

one of you from his iniquities." Acts 3:25-26.

Luke also records:

> *"But when the Jews saw the multitudes, they were filled with envy and spoke against those things which were spoken by Paul, contradicting and blaspheming. Then Paul and Barnabas waxed bold, and said, "IT WAS NE-CESSARY THAT THE WORD OF GOD SHOULD FIRST HAVE BEEN SPOKEN TO YOU; but seeing you put it from you and judge yourselves unworthy of everlasting life, we turn to the Gentiles." Acts 13:45-46.*

And WHY was it necessary that the Word of God should have to be spoken to the Jews first? (Are you beginning to see?)

Because the 70 weeks were not expired yet! Probation had not closed yet!

John wrote:

> *"He came unto His own, and His own (Israel) received Him not." John 1:11*

After the stoning of Stephen, the transgression was finished. Then Saul was blinded on the road to Damascus and the Lord spoke to Ananias,

> *"But the Lord said unto him, "Go your way: for he is a chosen vessel unto Me, to bear My name before the Gentiles and kings and the children of Israel." Acts 9:15*

Saul was converted on the road to Damascus from a persecutor to an apostle... the Apostle Paul who was sent to the Gentiles and

Jews.

Then the apostle Peter received his vision on the rooftop to erase his prejudice of the Gentiles, (Acts 10) which had to be done now that the gospel was to go to the Gentiles.

Peter went to Cornelius' house where others were gathered there and said,

> *"You know how it is an unlawful thing for a man that is a Jew to keep company or come unto one of another nation; but GOD HAS SHOWED ME THAT I SHOULD NOT CALL ANY MAN COMMON OR UNCLEAN." "Of a truth I perceive that GOD IS NO RESPECTER OF PERSONS: But in every nation he that fears Him and works righteousness, is accepted with Him." "When they heard these things, they held their peace and glorified God saying, "Then God also to the Gentiles granted repentance unto life." Acts 10:28, 34-35, 11:18.*

Let Us Move On.

> *"And in the midst (middle) of the week He shall cause the sacrifice and the oblation to cease,"*

Not only was Jesus crucified in the middle (midst) of the final week of the 70 week prophecy, but was also literally crucified in the middle of the week, on Wednesday.

The next portion is self-explanatory. Jesus fulfilled the type/antitype of animal sacrifices and offerings thus causing the sacrifice and oblation to cease. However, some may argue that the Jews rejected Jesus' claim to be Messiah and continued animal sacrifices, which is true, but it does not change the fact that God ushered in the "New Covenant."

In other words: It does not matter what the Jews did, Jesus still caused the sacrifice and oblation to be done away.

> *"Blotting out the handwriting of ordnances that was against us, which was contrary to us, and took it out of the way, nailing it to His cross." Colossians 2:14.*

> *"And for the overspreading of abominations He shall make it desolate, even until the consummation, and that determined shall be poured upon the desolate."*

This is how the passage ends, and while the next passage that I am going to share with you applied to the 1st temple's destruction, I think it is fitting to the destruction of the 2nd temple seeing that the LORD does not change...

> *"Moreover, all the chief of the priests, and the people transgressed very much after all the abominations of the heathen; and polluted the house of the LORD which He had hallowed in Jerusalem. And the LORD God of their fathers sent to them by His messengers, rising up be-times, and sending; because He had compassion on His people and on His dwelling place: But they mocked the messengers of God, and despised His words and misused His prophets, UNTIL THE WRATH OF THE LORD AROSE AGAINST HIS PEOPLE, TILL THERE WAS NO REMEDY." 2 Chronicles 36:14-16.*

Déjà Vu, All Over Again!

My hope is, by breaking down this prophecy for you line by line, you can start to see that the "church fathers" were just plain wrong about the Antichrist, and the 70 weeks of Daniel 9. However, there is another passage of scripture that needs to be explained as well. It concerns the "Man of Sin."

I will cover that in the next chapter.

Jesus Is The Messiah.

CHAPTER 10

THE MAN OF SIN

The church at Thessalonica received the letter from Paul which we call 1 Thessalonians and apparently thought that the 2nd Coming of Jesus was imminent. Paul had spoken of the "Day of the Lord" in that letter, and so he wrote a 2nd letter to strengthen the brethren, and to clear up the misunderstanding.

> *"Now we beseech you brethren, by the coming of our Lord Jesus Christ, and by our gathering together unto Him, that you be not soon shaken in mind or be troubled, neither by spirit nor by word, nor by letter as from us, as that the day of Christ is at hand. Let no man deceive you by any means: for that day shall not come except there comes a falling away first, and that MAN OF SIN be revealed, the son of perdition; who opposes and exalts himself above all that is called God, or that is worshipped; so that he as God sits in the temple of God, showing himself that he is God." 2 Thessalonians 2:1-4.*

The Man of Sin has been linked to an Antichrist figure since antiquity. Many of the church fathers also linked the Man of Sin to Daniel's little horn of Daniel 7 & 8, the Beast of Revelation 13, and the Whore of Babylon which rides on the Beast of Revelation 13.

Since Thessalonians does not give any clues as to who the Man of Sin is, and the book of Revelation gives many clues as to who the "Whore of Babylon" is and the Beast that she sits on, we will focus our attention there.

THE WHORE OF BABYLON

Revelation 17

"And there came one of the seven angels which had the seven vials, and talked with me, saying unto me, "Come here: I will show you the judgment of the great whore that sits upon many waters." Revelation 17:1

The Bible is an amazing Book and will explain itself if we let it.

"And he said unto me, "The waters which you saw, where the whore sits are peoples, and multitudes, and nations and tongues." Revelation 17:15

So, there is the first clue. The whore will have world-wide influence.

"With whom the kings of the earth have committed fornication and the inhabitants of the earth have been made drunk with the wine of her fornication." Revelation 17:2

Here is the second and third clues. The kings of the earth are "in bed" so-to-speak with her and the inhabitants of the earth are "made drunk" with her fornication.

"And the woman was arrayed in purple and scarlet color

and decked with gold and precious stones and pearls, having a golden cup in her hand full of abominations and filthiness of her fornication." Revelation 17:4

Here are more clues to the identity of the Whore of Babylon. Arrayed in purple and scarlet color. Decked with gold and precious stones and pearls and having the golden cup in her hand full of abominations and filthiness of her fornication.

Notice The Word: "Fornication" Keeps Coming Up?

There are many more clues as to who this world-wide entity is, but I will go ahead and tell you to end the suspense.

There are 2 women in the book of Revelation.

The woman of Revelation 12 which represents the True Church, and the woman of Revelation 17, the Whore of Babylon, which represents the False church.

So what church is arrayed in purple and scarlet color? The Catholic church.

What church covers up child molestation by its priests? The Catholic church.

What church has thousands of priceless treasures in its treasury? The Catholic church.

What church has made people so drunk with their "wine" that they just look the other way knowing that child molestation by their priests is ongoing? The Catholic church.

What church is world-wide and has enough influence that presidents and kings of nations seek an audience with the pope? The Catholic church.

"And here is the mind that has wisdom. The seven heads

are SEVEN MOUNTAINS, on which the woman sits." Revelation 17:9

What church sits upon seven mountains? The Catholic church. Google it.

New York, New York is known as the "Big Apple," Chicago, Illinois is known as the "Windy City," Dallas, Texas is known as the "Big D," and Rome, Italy is known as the "Eternal City" and sits upon 7 hills, Palatine hill, Aventine hill, Capitoline hill, Viminal hill, Esquiline hill, Caelian hill, and Quirinal hill. (There is only one Eternal City, Jerusalem).

Which church has its headquarters in Rome? The Catholic church.

The focus and scope of this book is not to educate you on the history of the Catholic church and all the abominations that they have committed in the past and continue to commit today. However, if you would like to educate yourself further just google: the Inquisition; Indulgences, death toll of the Inquisition, death toll of the crusades, triple crown of the papacy, the pope and the antichrist etc.

The abominations that the Catholic church have committed and the people that they have killed during the inquisition and the crusades have long been thought of as the fulfillment of Biblical prophecy, especially in the books of Daniel and Revelation.

The Protestant Reformation was started in 1517 by Martin Luther and his 95 thesis, which he nailed to the Castle Church door in Wittenberg, Germany. The 95 thesis was a document listing 95 abominable practices of the Catholic church. At number 21 of the list was the practice of asking payment, called "indulgences," for the forgiveness of sins, and most of the document deals with this practice. The church taught that if you gave money to the church as an "Indulgence" then your personal sins, past, present, and future would be forgiven and that your loved ones who have already died, would be released from purgatory and go straight to heaven.

Number 86 on the list is: "Why does not the pope, whose wealth is today greater than the wealth of the richest Crassus, build this one basilica of St. Peter with his own money rather than with the money of poor believers?"

The sale of Indulgences was to construct St. Peter's Basilica and that is how the church built it. I can certainly identify with Martin Luther's position here. I have often thought the same thing when I see Pastors beg for money knowing that they already have extreme personal wealth. (Do not misconstrue what I am saying though, tithing to a worthwhile cause or organization is what we are to do as Christians and the LORD blesses us for it).

The purpose and scope of this book is not to give commentary to all the passages of the books of Daniel and Revelation that deal with the so-called Antichrist, Man of Sin, or Little Horn power, but only give you enough information to be able to see that the mainstream doctrine of Antichrist and the Man of Sin is erroneous so that you won't be waiting for a 3rd Temple to be rebuilt and an Antichrist to take his seat in the Temple... In other words, people who have their minds cluttered with such false doctrines will not be able to see the truth about the extremely near return of Christ which will be presented in latter chapters of this writing. So, with that in mind let us move on to the Man of Sin.

The Man Of Sin

The verse in question is this one; from 2 Thessalonians 2:4,

> "Who opposes and exalts HIMSELF above all that is called God or that is worshipped; so that he as God sits in the temple of God, SHOWING HIMSELF THAT HE IS GOD."

The false doctrine is that sometime in the future, a man of sin (the antichrist) will take his seat in the newly constructed 3rd Temple in Jerusalem and masquerade as God Himself. I strongly disagree. For starters, as I have previously said, THE DOME OF THE ROCK, the 3rd most holy site in all of Islam currently sits in the exact location where a 3rd Temple would be built.

> Secondly, If the "man of sin" is to be associated with the beast of Revelation 13 and the Whore of Babylon of Revelation 17, then the man of sin must take his seat in Rome, not Jerusalem.

Google: "what is the holiest place on earth?" I just did. Do you know what was at the very top of the list? (#1) SAINT PETER'S BASILICA

Papal Infallibiity

The dogma was first drafted amid controversy by the First Vatican Council in 1870. The "PAPAL INFALLIBILITY" doctrine means that the Pope CANNOT ERR OR TEACH AN ERROR if he is speaking "EX CATHEDRA" or "FROM THE CHAIR" and is speaking on matters of morals and faith. IT IS STILL ROMAN CATHOLIC DOCTRINE TODAY!

Think about it! Use your own brain! Do not look down in the commentary of your study bible. Use your own common sense.

If the Pope thinks that ST. Peter's Basilica is the most holy place on earth, and if he thinks that he is infallible, then doesn't 2 Thessalonians 2:4 describe him EXACTLY?

> *"Who opposes and EXALTS HIMSELF above all that is called God, or that is worshipped; so that he as God SITS IN THE TEMPLE OF GOD SHOWING HIMSELF THAT HE IS GOD."*

There is only one human being who has ever lived that did not ERR. Jesus Christ. There is only one person who did not lie... Jesus Christ.

Did you notice the doctrine of infallibility stated that when he speaks "ex cathedra?" (From the chair).

And the man of sin SITS in the temple. It is no accident. Let me say again, IT'S NO ACCIDENT OR COINCIDENCE, (THE DEF-INITION OF COINCIDENCE IS: "WHEN GOD WANTS TO REMAIN ANONOMOUS").

Other Considerations

I could go on and on about Catholic doctrine saying that we can pray to Mary and several other saints to act as mediators be-tween us and God, when the bible clearly states that there is ONE MEDIATOR between us and God, Jesus Christ. (1 Timothy 2:5).

Or, how the Catholic church is the possessor of the "Keys of Peter" and supposedly has the authority to change Times and Laws, or even Scripture itself. Daniel 7:25.

Or how the beast of Revelation 13 had one of its heads receive a "deadly wound", but the deadly wound was healed... (Revelation 13:3)

This is speaking of Pope Pius VI. During the French Revolution-ary Wars, Napoleon's General, Berthier, took Pope Pius VI cap-tive and he died in captivity in 1799. But the deadly wound was healed when Pope Pius VII was crowned Pope. Google it.

I keep saying, "Google it," because I want you to be educated. To be able to grasp the most important revelations presented in this writing you need to know historical facts. It is because of a lack of knowledge that most "theologians" are "futurists" because it is much easier for the historically uneducated person to cast everything that they do not understand into the future and make up whatever scenario that seems appropriate. However, as for theologians of today, I think that many of them are just building upon the futuristic ideas that have been handed down to them through church "fathers" who lived so long ago that they did not have much choice as whether to be futurists or historicists. (Because there was no history to compare scripture with).

We have the advantage here in 2021 (the date of this writing) to look back nearly 2 millennia to the crucifixion and be able to match prophecy with prophecy fulfilled. Let me say that again, for it is important; WE HAVE THE ADVANTAGE HERE IN 2021 TO LOOK BACK NEARLY 2 MILLENNIA TO THE CRUCIFIXION AND BE ABLE TO MATCH PROPHECY WITH PROPHECY FULFILLED.

So why would any "theologian" now-a-days, take the futurists method of exegesis over the historicist method? (Does not make sense to me either).

Let us move on to the main point of this book:

The return of Jesus.

Jesus Is The Chief Cornerstone Of The Temple.

Jesus Is The Truth, And The Life.

CHAPTER 11

THE DISPENSATION

The "synoptic" gospels are Matthew, Mark and Luke, because of their similar content. All three gospels record an account of Jesus coming to the other "side" of Galilee and approaching a man with demons. Luke 8: 26-40, Mark 5:1-20, Matthew 8:29-34.

> *"And when He was come to the other side into the country of the Gergesenes, there met Him two possessed with devils, coming out of the tombs, exceeding fierce, so that no man might pass by that way. And behold they cried out, saying, "What have we to do with you Jesus, you Son of God? HAVE YOU COME HERE TO TORMENT US BEFORE THE TIME?" Matthew 8:28-29*

Hello? The Demons Knew That Jesus Was Early!

<u>They knew that there was a time allotted for the Second Coming of Jesus and that He was 2000 years early</u>! How could they know that He was early? Because the devil and his fallen angels know scripture... that is how.

When Jesus was tempted by the devil in Matthew 4, it became apparent that he (the devil) knows scripture. Notice that they also knew who He was, while most of the religious leaders of that time did not.

> *"Then was Jesus led up of the Spirit into the wilderness to be tempted of the devil. And when He had fasted forty days and forty nights, He was afterward hungry. And when the tempter came to Him, he said, "If you be the Son of God, command that these stones be made bread." But He answered and said, "It is written, Man shall not live by bread alone, but by every word that proceeds out of the mouth of God." (Deuteronomy 8:3b). Then the devil takes Him up into the holy city, and sits Him on a pinnacle of the temple, and said to Him, "If you be the Son of God cast yourself down: FOR IT IS WRITTEN, He shall give His angels charge concerning you: and in their hands they shall bear you up, lest at any time you dash your foot against a stone." (Psalm 91:11-12). Jesus said to him, "It is written again, you shall not tempt the LORD your God." (Deuteronomy 6:16). Again, the devil takes Him up into an exceeding high mountain, and shows Him all the kingdoms of the world, and the glory of them; and says to Him, "All these things will I give you, if you will fall down and worship me." Then Jesus said to him, "Get you hence, Satan: for it is written, you shall worship the LORD your God, and Him only shall you serve." (Exodus 34:14). Matthew 4:1-10.*

It becomes clear that the adversary knows Scripture, and hopefully you will also see the "Time Allotted" for the end of all things as we know them.

The Scriptures point us repeatedly to the end of this current dispensation.

> *"That in the dispensation of the FULLNESS OF TIMES He might gather together in one all things in Christ, both*

which are in heaven, and which are on earth, even in Him." Ephesians 1:10.

God commands men everywhere to repent, "Because He has APPOINTED A DAY, in which He will judge the world in righteousness by that Man whom He has ordained; whereof He has given assurance unto all men, in that He has raised Him from the dead." Acts 17:31

"(God) has made of one blood all nations of men to dwell on all the face of the earth and HAS DETERMINED THE TIMES BEFORE APPOINTED." Acts 17:26

"For the vision is yet for an APPOINTED TIME..." Habakkuk 2:3.

"For the end shall be AT THE TIME APPOINTED." Daniel 11:27b.

"And some of them of understanding shall fall, to try them, and to purge, and to make them white, even to the time of the end; because it is yet FOR A TIME APPOINTED." Daniel 11:35.

Daniel heard God speaking to Gabriel. God told Gabriel to make Daniel understand the vision which he was given,

"So he (Gabriel) came near where I stood: and when he

came, I was afraid, and fell on my face: but he said unto me, "Understand, O son of man; for AT THE TIME OF THE END shall be the vision." Now as he was speaking with me, I was in a deep sleep on my face toward the ground: but he touched me and set me upright. And he said, "Behold, I will make you know what shall be in the LAST END of the indignation: FOR AT THE TIME AP-POINTED THE END SHALL BE." Daniel 8:17-19.

As previously pointed out in the Introduction of this book, I do not know the day or the hour of Jesus' return... No one does, only The Father knows. But there is a time APPOINTED.

Many times, the scriptures refer to Christ's 2nd coming as: THE DAY OF THE LORD, THE LAST DAY, THE DAY OF REDEMPTION, THE DAY OF OUR LORD JESUS, or simply THE DAY...

The Last Day

Jesus said, "Whosoever eats My flesh, and drinks My blood has eternal life; and I will raise him up at THE LAST DAY." John 6:54.

"And this is the Father's will which has sent Me, that of all which He has given Me I should lose nothing but should raise it up again AT THE LAST DAY." John 6:39

"And this is the will of Him that sent Me that everyone which sees the Son and believes on Him, may have ever-lasting life: and I will raise him up AT THE LAST DAY." John 6:40.

"No man can come to Me except the Father which has sent Me draw him: and I will raise him up AT THE LAST DAY." John 6:44.

"He that rejects Me, and receives not My words, has one that judges him: the Word that I have spoken, the same shall judge him IN THE LAST DAY."

Do you get the point? There is a DAY appointed. Paul wrote of it in this way:

"Being confident of this very thing that He which has begun a good work in you will perform it until THE DAY OF JESUS CHRIST." Philippians 1:6.

"And this I pray, that your love may abound yet more and more in knowledge and in all judgment; that you may approve things that are excellent; that you may be sincere and without offence till THE DAY OF CHRIST." Philippians 1:9-10.

"Let no corrupt communication proceed out of your mouth, but that which is good to the use of edifying, that it may minister grace unto the hearers. And grieve not the Holy Spirit of God, whereby you are sealed until THE DAY OF REDEMPTION." Ephesians 4:29-30.

I could go on and on, but I think there is enough evidence to understand that there is a time period allotted for this existence as we know it and that it will come to an end at the coming of Christ.

One especially important point that I would like to make at this juncture is: Do not believe the false doctrine that Christians cannot see the day of the Lord approaching. If that were true, why would the author of Hebrews write this:

> *"And let us consider one another to provoke unto love and to good works; Not forsaking the assembling of ourselves together, as the manner of some is, but exhorting one another: and so much the more, as you SEE THE DAY APPROACHING." Hebrews 10:24-25.*

The pulpits across the United States of America, for the most part, have fallen asleep, or are in a slumber as to the signs of the times. I do not suppose it is any different worldwide. Jesus warned of this spiritual slumber:

> *"And as it was in the days of Noah, so shall it be also in the days of the Son of man. They did eat, they drank, they married wives they were given in marriage until the day that Noah entered the ark, and the flood came, and destroyed them all. Likewise, also as it was in the days of Lot: They did eat, they drank, they bought, they sold, they planted, they builded; but the same day that Lot went out of Sodom it rained fire and brimstone from heaven and destroyed them all. Even so shall it be in THE DAY when the Son of man is revealed. In THAT DAY, he which shall be upon the housetop, and his stuff in the house, let him not come down to take it away: and he that is in the field, let him likewise not return back. Remember Lot's wife. Whosoever shall seek to save his life shall lose it; and who-*

soever shall lose his life shall preserve it. I tell you, in that night there shall be two in one bed; the one shall be taken, and the other shall be left. Two women shall be grinding together: the one shall be taken, and the other left. Two men shall be in the field; the one shall be taken, and the other left." Luke 17:26-36.

Imagine what it was like in the days of Noah. Noah was a just man and feared God, so the LORD chose him to build a huge boat (ark) to save enough animals to repopulate the earth. When he started building the ark, I can just imagine what his neighbors must have thought. They probably thought he was insane. The fact that only Noah and his wife and his 3 sons and their wives were saved speaks volumes to the notion that no one else believed Noah enough to help in the building of such an enormous project. Surely, if he had outside help, they would have been included in the roster. So, I can imagine the ridicule that Noah and his family must have endured.

Even today, people who try to warn of God's impending judgement and urgency of repentance are relegated to the image of a homeless insane person holding a sign warning of impending doom. Do not be that person who is poking fun at the messenger of impending doom.

Another point that should be elaborated upon is Lot's wife and Lot's sons-in-law. Lot was told by the 2 Angels to gather up his family so Lot went to his daughters' husbands and told them to get ready to leave because the city was about to be destroyed.

> *"But he seemed as one who mocked unto his sons in law."*
> *Genesis 19:14b.*

The Hebrew word translated "mocked" is: TSACHAQ and means: "to play, to sport, to jest..." In other words, the sons in law thought Lot was "just playing" with them, they did not believe him... So, they perished.

Lot's wife perished for a different reason. The Angels warned:

> *"And it came to pass, when they had brought them forth abroad, that he said, "Escape for your life; LOOK NOT BEHIND YOU, neither stay in the plain: escape to the mountain lest you be consumed." Genesis 19:17.*

Lot's wife looked behind her, back at the city and was turned to a pillar of salt. She cared more for the possessions she was leaving behind and her old life than her salvation. Do not be as Lot's wife or Lot's sons in law.

> *Whosoever shall seek to save his life shall lose it; and whosoever shall lose his life shall preserve it.*

Jesus Is Our Hope And Glory.

CHAPTER 12

THE RAPTURE

Another point to cover is the false teaching of the RAPTURE. The word "Rapture" appears nowhere in scripture. There are several views on the term "Rapture" and for those who say that it refers to the Second Coming of Christ and believers being "caught up" together with Him according to 1 Thessalonians 4:16-17, I share your view.

However, to those who have been taught to accept the false teaching that there will be a "secret rapture" or 2nd coming and then a 3rd Coming of Jesus; or to those who hold the belief that one day half of all people on earth will be "raptured" away and disappear leaving behind (alive) those that have not accepted Christ as their Savior, I take issue.

> This is not what the Scriptures or Jesus Himself taught.

One of the main culprits of spreading the false doctrine of the Rapture have been authors in recent decades, who started with one book of fiction dealing with the subject and then spinning off numerous sequels to that first book, creating an entire series of books.

The authors and the books will remain unnamed in this writing because I do not want to open myself up to a lawsuit. I have better things to do with the rest of my life than sit in a courtroom.

However, I will say this: People are gullible, they read a work of fiction for entertainment and because there is some essence of truth covered in the writing it makes the lies a bit more palatable. It is the same formula the devil used in the Garden of Eden to entice Eve to sin. First, he cast doubt upon what God had said,

"Has God said, you shall not eat of every tree of the garden?" (Casting doubt) Eve answered, "we may eat of the fruit of the trees of the garden: But of the fruit of the tree which is in the midst of the garden God said, you shall not eat of it, lest you die." And the serpent said, "You shall not surely die (LIE) For God does know that in the day you eat thereof, then your eyes shall be opened (TRUTH) and you shall be as gods (LIE) knowing good and evil (TRUTH)." Genesis 3:1b-5.

Satan works the same way today. His modus operandi has not changed. And what is worse is that "his ministers" masquerade as "ministers of righteousness." 2 Corinthians 11:13-15.

The passage towards the end of Luke 17 says "one will be taken, the other will be left," (3 times) and the verse that commentators frequently omit is the last verse of Luke 17:

"And they (the disciples) answered and said unto Him, "Where, Lord?" (Where are the ones left behind? Remember the context of leaving Sodom and Gomorrah in v.32 and 33 the ones taken will escape destruction, the ones left behind, will not. They will become buzzard food) Wherever the body is, there will the eagles be gathered together." Luke 17:37.

The Greek word translated EAGLES is: AETOS and means eagle, (from its wind like flight). The root word of "Aetos" had only to do with the "wind" aspect and not with the species of bird. So,

I looked up AETOS in Thayer's Greek-English Lexicon and discovered Job 39:27-30

"Does the eagle mount up at Your command, and make her nest on high? She dwells and abides on the rock, upon the crag of the rock, and the strong place. From there she seeks the prey, and her eyes behold afar off. Her young ones also suck up blood: and WHERE THE SLAIN ARE, THERE IS SHE."

Once again scripture explains scripture. The people "left behind" are slain… bird food, dead, they are not looking around wondering where everyone went.

A parallel passage is in Matthew 24:27-28

"For as the lightening comes out of the East and shines to the West; so, shall also the coming of the Son of man be. For wheresoever the CARCASE IS, THERE WILL THE EAGLES BE GATHERED TOGETHER."

The doctrine of a "Secret Rapture" is FALSE. His coming will be as lightning streaking across the sky which is very visible and what does lightening do? It makes THUNDER so it will be LOUD as well.

"Wherefore if they shall say unto you "Behold, He is in the desert; go not forth: behold He is in the SECRET chambers; believe it not" Matthew 24:26.

Proponents of the "Rapture" doctrine use Revelation 3:10 to try and back up their theory,

"Because you have kept the word of my patience, I also will keep you from the hour of temptation, which shall come upon all the world, to try them that dwell upon the earth."

Well, I guess if I pulled a verse here and a verse there from the Bible without harmonizing the entirety of scripture, then I could make the Bible say just about anything. But Jesus warned of persecution. Paul warned of not falling away when tried.

God is saying that there will be those whom He will not "test." There is a play on words here. The Greek word translated "TRY" is the root word for the Greek word translated "TEMPTATION." Temptation = PEIRASMOS a putting to proof (by experiment {of good}, experience {of evil}, by implication adversity. TRY = PEIRAZO to test, i.e., endeavor, scrutinize, entice, discipline.

A study of the Greek reveals that some will be kept from the "fiery trial" that is to come but it will not be universal. <u>And nothing in the original language suggests that God will REMOVE those people FROM the trials only that He will KEEP them THROUGH the trials</u>.

This can also be discerned by what Peter wrote:

"Beloved think it not strange concerning the FIERY TRIAL, WHICH IS TO TRY YOU, as though some strange thing happened unto you: But rejoice, inasmuch as you are partakers of Christ's sufferings; that, when His glory shall be revealed you may be glad also with exceeding joy." 1 Peter 4:12-13.

In Matthew 13 Jesus puts forth the parable of the Sower. Then He explains the parable.

After this, "Another parable He put forth to them, saying, "The kingdom of heaven is like a man which sowed good seed in his field: But while men slept, his enemy came and sowed tares (weeds) among the wheat, and went his way. But when the blade was sprung up and brought forth fruit then appeared the tares also. So, the servants of the householder came and said unto him, "Sir, didn't you sow good seed in your field? Why then does it have tares?" He said unto them, "An enemy has done this." The servants said, "Do you want us to go and gather them up?" But he said, "No; lest while you gather up the tares you root up also the wheat with them. LET BOTH GROW TOGETHER UNTIL THE HARVEST: and in the time of harvest, I will say to the reapers, "Gather together FIRST THE TARES and bind them in bundles to burn them: but gather the wheat into my barn." Matthew 13:24-30

After the parable of the tares, Jesus told another parable.

"Then Jesus sent the multitude away and went into the house: and His disciples came to Him, saying, "Declare to us the parable of the tares of the field." He answered and said to them, "He that sows the good seed is the Son of man; The field is the world; the good seed are the children of the kingdom; but the tares are the children of the wicked one; The enemy that sowed them is the devil; the harvest is the end of the world; and the reapers are the angels. As therefore the tares are gathered and burned in the fire; so, shall it be in the end of this world. The Son of man (Jesus) shall send forth His angels, and they shall gather out of His kingdom all things that offend, and them which do iniquity; and shall cast them into a furnace of fire: there shall be wailing and gnashing of teeth, then shall the righteous shine forth as the sun in the king-

dom of their Father. WHO HAS EARS TO HEAR LET HIM HEAR." Matthew 13:36-43.

Let me ask you a question: Do you have ears to hear? Did Jesus say ANYTHING about taking the wheat first, then sending teachers to educate the tares to hopefully get them to turn from their evil ways? No, He did not. He very plainly explained that the world as we know it will continue until the destroying angels are sent to burn up the tares.

> *"For behold, the day is coming, that shall burn as an oven; and all the proud, yes and all that do wickedly, shall be stubble: and the day that comes shall burn them up, says the LORD of hosts, that it shall leave them neither root nor branch. But unto you that fear My name shall the Sun of righteousness arise with healing in His wings; and you shall go forth and grow up as calves of the stall. And you shall tread down the wicked; for they shall be ashes under the soles of your feet in the day that I shall do this, says the LORD of hosts." Malachi 4:1-3*

> *"The Lord is not slack concerning His promise as some men count slackness; but is longsuffering to us, not willing that any should perish, but that all should come to repentance. But the day of the LORD will come as a thief in the night in the which the heavens shall pass away with a great noise and the elements shall melt with fervent heat, the earth also and the works that are therein shall be burned up. Seeing then that all these things shall be dissolved what manner of persons ought you to be in all holy conversation and godliness, looking for and hasting unto the coming of the day of God, wherein the heavens being on fire shall be dissolved, and the elements shall*

melt with fervent heat? Nevertheless we, according to His promise, look for new heavens and a new earth, wherein dwells righteousness." 2Peter 3:9-13.

Peter says that the "elements" will melt with fervent heat... (twice). What is made of elements? EVERYTHING.

David says it like this:

"A fire goes before Him and burns up His enemies round about. His lightnings enlightened the world: the earth saw, and trembled. THE HILLS MELTED LIKE WAX at the presence of the LORD, at the presence of the Lord of the whole earth." Psalms 97:3-5.

Enoch describes it similarly,

"The words of the blessing of Enoch wherewith he blessed the elect and righteous, who will be living in the day of tribulation, when all the wicked and godless are to be removed. And he took up his parable and said "Enoch a righteous man, whose eyes were opened by God, saw the vision of the Holy One in the heavens, which the angels showed me and from them I heard everything, and from them I understood as I saw, but not for this generation, but for a remote one which is to come. Concerning the elect, I said and took up my parable concerning them: The Holy Great One will come forth from His dwelling, and the eternal God will tread upon the earth, (even) on Mount Sinai, and appear in the strength of His might from the heaven of heavens. And all shall be smitten with fear, and the Watchers (fallen angels) shall quake, and great fear and trembling shall seize them unto the ends of the earth. And the high mountains shall be shaken, and the high hills shall be made low, and shall MELT LIKE WAX before

the flame. And the earth shall be wholly rent in sunder, and all that is upon the earth shall perish and there shall be a judgement upon all (men). But with the righteous He will make peace and will protect the elect, and mercy shall be upon them. And they shall be prospered, and they shall all be blessed. And He will help them all and light shall appear unto them, and He will make peace with them. And behold! He comes with ten thousands of His holy ones to execute judgement upon all, and to destroy all the ungodly: and to convict all flesh of all the works of their ungodliness which they have ungodly committed, and of all the hard things which ungodly sinners have spoken against Him." The book of 1 Enoch 1:1-9.

I know that some of the readers of this book may have been taught to not read anything but the approved "canon" of Scripture (66 books) ... but let me ask those of you that hold on to that view. If it is good enough for Jude to quote it (Jude 14&15) why is it not good enough for you to read it?

Notice this, and then we will move on: Jesus, Peter, David, the book of Malachi, and Enoch, and many more witnesses that we did not cover, attest to the fact that the day of the Lord will be a day of gloom and doom for many but for the elect, the day that we have patiently waited for.

> THERE WILL NOT BE A "RAPTURE" OF THE RIGHTEOUS BEFORE THE DESTRUCTION OF THE WICKED. Period.

Jesus Is He That Sows The Good Seed.

CHAPTER 13

THE FIG TREE

"The Lord is not slack concerning His promise, as some men count slackness, but is longsuffering towards us, not willing that any should perish, but that all should come to repentance." 2 Peter 3:9.

G od has given us a promise. "In my Father's house are many mansions: if it were not so, I would have told you, I will come again, and receive you unto Myself; that where I am, there you may be also." John 14:2-3.

In the latter days of this existence, we are warned of false teachers while waiting for the "promise" of Jesus' return.

"Knowing this first, that there shall come in the last days scoffers (false teachers), walking after their own lusts, and saying, "Where is the promise of His coming? For since the fathers fell asleep, all things continue as they were from the beginning of the creation." For this they willingly are ignorant of, that by the Word of God the heavens were of old, and the earth standing out of the water and in the water: Whereby the world that then was, being overflowed with water, perished: But the heavens and the earth which are now, by the same Word are kept in store, reserved unto fire against the day of judgment and perdition of ungodly men." 2 Peter 3:3-7.

God has given us many promises. The promises of a wonderful place in the New Jerusalem, and the approaching return of our Savior and of course, the forgiveness of sins, top the list.

Jesus has also given us "signs" to look for concerning His second coming and the end of this age.

"As for these things which you behold, the days will come, in which there shall not be left one stone upon another, that shall not be thrown down. (Speaking of the destruction of the Temple). And they (His disciples) asked Him saying, "Master, but when shall these things be? And what SIGN will there be when these things shall come to pass?" And He said, "Take heed that you be not deceived: for many shall come in My name saying, "I am Christ; and the time draws near," go not therefore after them. But when you shall hear of wars and commotions, be not terrified: for these things must first come to pass; but the end is not by and by." Then He said to them, "Nation shall rise against nation and kingdom against kingdom: And great earthquakes shall be in various places, and famines, and pestilences; and fearful sights and great signs shall there be from heaven. But before all these, they shall lay their hands on you and persecute you, delivering you up to the synagogues, and into prisons being brought before kings and rulers for My name's sake. And it shall turn to you for a testimony. Settle it therefore in your hearts, not to meditate before what you shall answer: For I will give you a mouth and wisdom, which all your adversaries shall not be able to gainsay nor resist. And you shall be hated of all men for my namesake. But there shall not a hair of your head perish. In your patience possess you your souls. And when you shall see Jerusalem compassed with armies, then know that the desolation thereof is near. Then let them which are in Judea flee to the mountains; and let them which are in the middle of it depart out; and let not

them that are in the countries enter therein. For these are the days of vengeance, that all things which are written may be fulfilled. But woe unto them that are with child, and to them that give suck in those days! For there shall be great distress in the land, and wrath upon these people. And they shall fall by the edge of the sword and shall be led away captive into all nations; and Jerusalem shall be trodden down of the Gentiles, until the times of the Gentiles be fulfilled. And there shall be signs in the sun, and in the moon, and in the stars; and upon the earth distress of nations, with perplexity; and the sea and the waves roaring; men's hearts failing them for fear, and for looking after those things which are coming on the earth; For the powers of heaven shall be shaken. And then shall they see the Son of man coming in a cloud with power and great glory. And when these things begin to come to pass then look up and lift up your heads for your redemption draws near. And He spoke to them a parable, "behold the fig tree and all the trees when they now shoot forth you see and know of your own selves that summer is now near at hand. So likewise, when you see these things come to pass, know that the Kingdom of God is near at hand. Verily I say into you, this generation shall not pass away, till all be fulfilled. Heaven and earth shall pass away but My words shall not pass away." Luke 21:6-33.

The destruction of Jerusalem and the Temple in 70 AD by the Roman army commanded by the General, Titus, is a fact of history and so is the dispersion of the Jewish peoples and the persecution they endured; so, for the purpose of this writing we will turn our attention to the time period that pertains to us… Until the 'TIMES OF THE GENTILES' be fulfilled.

Notice that Jesus says that there will be SIGNS in the Sun, Moon, and stars. "Blood" moons have been appearing at increasing rates it seems. May 26, 2021, was the last occurrence at the time of this writing, and it was also a lunar eclipse. There were 2 in 2020. On June 10, 2021, there will be a sunrise in which the sun will be partially eclipsed... they are calling it: "red devils" horns..." Google it. You cannot make this stuff up any better.

For the "distress of nations" one only must turn on a newscast. Tsunamis, hurricanes and cyclones are all increasing in occurrences and intensity according to the weather service... Then He speaks of the powers of heaven being shaken and of His return to this earth... then He told the Parable of the "FIG TREE." In the parallel passage in Matthew, He tells us to "LEARN" the Parable of the FIG TREE. Matthew 24:32-34.

So, let us identify what, or who the Fig Tree is in Gods eyes, according to Scripture.

> *"I found Israel like grapes in the wilderness; I saw your fathers as the first ripe in the FIG TREE." Hosea 9:10a*

> *"The LORD showed me, and behold, two baskets of FIGS were set before the temple of the LORD... one basket had very good figs even like the figs that are first ripe, and the other basket had very naughty figs, which could not be eaten they were so bad... Thus says the LORD, the God of Israel; Like these good figs, so will I acknowledge them that are carried away captive of Judah... And as the evil figs, which cannot be eaten, they are so evil; surely thus says the LORD, So I will give Zedekiah the king of Judah, and his princes, and the residue of Jerusalem, that remain in this land and them that dwell in the land of Egypt; and I will deliver them to be removed into all the kingdoms of the earth for their hurt, to be a reproach and a proverb, a taunt and a curse, in all places where I shall drive them." Jeremiah 24: 1a,2,5a,8-9.*

Good figs or bad, Israel is the FIG TREE in Gods eyes.

Why is this important? To identify Israel as the Fig Tree?

Because of what follows:

> *"When his branch is yet tender and puts forth leaves, you know that summer is near: So likewise, when you shall see all these things, know that it is near, EVEN AT THE DOORS. Truly, I say unto you, THIS GENERATION SHALL NOT PASS UNTIL ALL THESE THINGS BE FULFILLED." Matthew 24:32-34.*

Israel as a nation with a homeland, ceased to exist from 70 AD until 1948 AD. It was a LOOONG Winter. But in 1917 the Balfour Declaration was drafted by England which opened the door for Israel to be declared an independent state with David Ben-Gurion as Prime Minister in 1948.

The long winter ended with the FIG TREE putting forth leaves once again and coming back to life. Jesus said that THIS GENERATION would not pass until all these things were fulfilled...

So, a person born in 1948 would be 83 years old in 2031. (2000 years after Jesus' crucifixion/resurrection).

This is one of the many ways that Scripture tells us the time allotted for Christ's return. But remember, this time period will be cut short for the ELECT'S SAKE. Matthew 24:22b.

Israel Is The Fig Tree.

Jesus Is Coming Soon!

CHAPTER 14

THE EXODUS

The Exodus of the Children of Israel from bondage (slavery) in Egypt is one of the best and most fascinating stories ever told. From the plagues in Egypt, to the miraculous crossing of the Red Sea, to the Bread coming down from heaven, the Exodus story has captured the imagination of countless souls for the past three millennia. And for good reason. The God of the Israelites, Yahweh, wanted His name proclaimed throughout the entire earth. So, He did many miraculous things in the process of delivering His People.

> *"For the scripture says unto Pharaoh, "Even for this same purpose have I raised you up, that I might show My power in you, and that My Name might be declared throughout all the earth." Romans 9:17 Exodus 9:16.*

Aside from His Name being declared throughout the earth, there was also another story being told in "type." In this chapter we will discover that story.

The Exodus story begins with Moses. In "type" Moses represents the "Law" for several reasons. The LORD gave Moses the 10 Commandments, the 2 tables of stone, on Mt. Sinai. Also, Moses was the author of the first 5 books of the bible commonly referred to as "The Law." Thus, at what is called "The Transfiguration," Moses represented the law, Elijah the prophets, and Jesus the

"New and Living Way." Mark 9.

Moses was also the forerunner of Christ for many reasons. At the time of the birth of Moses the King of Egypt spoke to the Hebrew midwives, and said,

> *"When you do the office of a midwife to the Hebrew women, and see them upon the stools; if it be a son, then you shall kill him: but if it be a daughter, then she shall live... And Pharaoh charged all his people, saying, "Every son that is born you shall cast into the river, and every daughter you shall save alive." Exodus 1:16,22.*

At the time of Jesus' birth: "The angel of the Lord appeared to Joseph in a dream saying,

> *"Arise and take the young child and His mother and flee into Egypt and stay there until I bring you word: for Herod will seek the young child to destroy Him." When he arose, he took the young child and His mother by night and departed into Egypt: And was there until the death of Herod: that it might be fulfilled which was spoken of the LORD by the prophet, saying, "Out of Egypt have I called My Son." (Hosea 11:1) Then Herod, when he saw that he was mocked of the wise men, was exceeding wroth (mad) and sent forth and slew all the children that were in Bethlehem, and in all the coasts thereof, from two years old and under, according to the time which he had diligently inquired of the wise men." Matthew 2:13-16.*

Evil forces were at work trying to destroy both children, but God intervened as He often does.

Moses was ultimately raised in the King of Egypt's house and when he was grown, he received his call from God at the burning bush...

> *"And the Angel of the LORD appeared unto him in a flame of fire out of the midst of a Bush; and he looked, and behold, the Bush burned with fire, and the Bush was not consumed. And Moses said, "I will now turn aside, and see this great sight why the Bush is not burnt." And when the Lord saw that he turned aside to see; God called unto him out of the midst of the Bush and said, "Moses, Moses." And he said, "Here I am." And He said, "Don't draw near to here, put off your shoes from your feet, for the place where you are standing is holy ground." Moreover, He said, "I am the God of your father, the God of Abraham, the God of Isaac, and the God of Jacob." And Moses hid his face; For he was afraid to look upon God. And the LORD said, "I have surely seen the affliction of my people which are in Egypt, and have heard their cry by reason of their taskmasters; For I know their sorrows; And I have come down to deliver them out of the hand of the Egyptians, and to bring them up out of that land unto a good land and a large, unto a land flowing with milk and honey; Unto the place of the Canaanites, and the Hittites, and the Amorites, and the Perizzites, and the Hivites, and the Jebusites. Now therefore, behold, the cry of the children of Israel is coming unto Me; and I have also seen the oppression wherewith the Egyptians oppress them. Come now therefore and I will send you unto Pharaoh, that you may bring forth my people the children of Israel out of Egypt." And Moses said to God, "Who am I, that I should go to Pharaoh, and that I should bring forth the children of Israel out of Egypt?" Exodus 3:2-11.*

Moses began making excuses, not wanting to answer God's call. And who could blame him? After all, he was hiding out in Midian after killing an Egyptian. Pharoah heard about the murder and sought to slay Moses, so his hesitancy to return to Pharoah is understandable.

So, he continued with more excuses to not be the LORD'S messenger:

"And Moses answered and said, "But behold, they will not believe me, nor listen to my voice: for they will say, "The LORD has not appeared unto you." Exodus 4:1

"And Moses said unto the LORD, "O my Lord, I am not eloquent, neither before this time, nor since you have spoken to your servant; FOR I AM SLOW OF SPEECH, AND OF A SLOW TONGUE." Exodus 4:10.

God ultimately gave Moses his brother Aaron to speak for him. Much speculation has been passed down over the millennia as to why Moses was slow of speech. Did he stutter? Did he stammer or have some other speech impediment? The answer to these questions can be found in the book of Jasher (which is referred to in our Bible as authoritative at Joshua 10:13 and 2 Samuel 1:18).

In chapter 70 of that book, it tells the story of a banquet in the Kings house with baby Moses seated beside the King of Egypt. Moses reached over and pulled the crown off the Kings head and placed it upon his own. The Kings magicians and counsellors cry out that the baby Moses should be put to death because it is a sign that Moses will take away Pharaoh's kingdom when he is grown. But the Angel of the LORD was there as well and proposed a test to see if the baby Moses did this thing with knowledge. The test was to bring a hot, live coal and an onyx stone and place them before the baby. If Moses reached for the onyx, then they would know that he acted with knowledge, but if he chose the burning coal then his life would be spared.

So, the King ordered that the onyx and the live coal be brought before Moses. They presented them to the baby and just as Moses was reaching for the onyx the Angel of the LORD guided his hand to the burning coal... and as babies often do, he put the hot coal in his mouth and burned his lips and tongue. That is why he could not speak well.

God also told Moses to remove his shoes because he was standing on Holy Ground. Why was this?

Answer: The mountain represented God Himself... the Father.

> *"Now Moses kept the flock of Jethro his father-in-law, the priest of Midian: and he led the flock to the backside of the desert, and came to THE MOUNTAIN OF GOD, even to Horeb." Exodus 3:1.*

We have already learned that Jesus was the "Rock at Horeb." 1 Corinthians 10:4. So, if you can visualize in your mind's eye, THE MOUNTAIN represents the Father... At the LORD'S presence the mountain quaked... A boulder dislodged from the mountain and rolled to the bottom and became the ROCK AT HOREB... representing the SON. When one looks at it in this way many difficult passages of Scripture are cleared up.

Such as:

> *"I and My Father are one." John 10:30*

> *"My Father is greater than I." John 14:28b.*

How can both statements be true? They are both made by Jesus. Think about the Mountain and the Rock. Isn't the Rock a piece of the Mountain which was PART OF the Mountain before the quake? Yes, So the statement "I and My Father are ONE, is true.

How about the other statement, "My Father is GREATER THAN I? Isn't that true as well? THE MOUNTAIN IS GREATER THAN THE ROCK. (Even though they are the same substance). This analogy also explains how Jesus was "brought forth" (not created)

> *"The LORD possessed Me in the beginning of His Way before His works of old. I was set up from everlasting from the beginning or ever the earth was. When there were no depths, I WAS BROUGHT FORTH, when there were no fountains abounding with water. Before the mountains were settled, before the hills, was I BROUGHT FORTH: While as yet He had not made the earth nor the fields nor the highest part of the dust of the world. When He prepared the heavens, I was there: When He set a compass upon the face of the depth: When He established the clouds above: When he strengthened the fountains of the deep: When He gave to the sea His decree, that the waters should not pass His commandment: When He appointed the foundations of the earth: Then I was by Him, as one brought up with Him: and I was daily His delight rejoicing always before Him." Proverbs 8:22-30.*

Think of it this way: Yahweh took a piece of Himself and separated it into the preincarnate Jesus. (Brought forth a piece of Himself).

This analogy of the ROCK is carried into the interpretation of the Kings dream of Daniel 2... The King of Babylon had dreamed a dream and could not recall the dream, so he asked his wise men to tell him the interpretation of the dream. Of course, his wise men could not because the King could not even tell them what he dreamt. But Daniel told the King that there is a God in Heaven who reveals secrets, and then told the King the dream and the interpretation.

"You O King saw and beheld a great image, this great image, whose brightness was excellent, stood before you and the form thereof was terrible. This image's head was of fine gold, his breast and his arms of silver, his belly and his thighs of brass, His legs of iron, his feet part of iron and part of clay. You saw until THAT A STONE WAS CUT OUT WITHOUT HANDS, which smote the image upon his feet that were of iron and clay and broke them to pieces. Then was the iron, the clay, the brass, the silver, and the gold, broken to pieces together, and became like the chaff of the summer threshing floors; and the wind carried them away, that no place was found for them: and THE STONE THAT SMOTE THE IMAGE BECAME A GREAT MOUNTAIN, and filled the whole earth. Forasmuch as you saw that THE STONE WAS CUT OUT OF THE MOUNTAIN WITHOUT HANDS and that it broke in pieces the iron, the brass, the clay, the silver, and the gold: the Great God has made known to the king what shall come to pass hereafter: and the dream is certain, and the interpretation thereof sure." Daniel 2:31-35,45.

Jesus IS the Stone... The Rock at Horeb, the Mountain of God.

Back to Moses and the Exodus...

The LORD put 10 plagues upon Egypt before Pharoah would let the children of Israel go. They were: Blood, Frogs, Lice, Flies, Cattle pestilence, Boils, Hail, Locusts, Darkness, and the death of all the Firstborn which finally resulted in the release of the children of Israel. Exodus chapters 7-11.

The death of the Firstborn prefigured or was a "type" of the death of Gods only Son Jesus. So is the Passover which was instituted the same night that the destroying angel came through the land of Egypt. The Israelites were told to sacrifice a lamb which was also a "type" of Jesus. Exodus 11 & 12.

Once the lamb was sacrificed, the Israelites were released from bondage which is a "type" of us accepting the grace of God, made available as a gift by the sacrifice of His Son, and so we too can be released from the bondage of Sin.

Once the Sacrifice is accepted, we are to be Baptized, just as Israel was "Baptized" in the cloud and Sea. Exodus 14, 1 Corinthians 10:1-2.

Then we are to feed on the Bread of Life, daily. The MAN/GOD Jesus, (the Word). Exodus 16, John 6.

We are to drink from the ROCK. Exodus 17, John 4:10-14.

Are you starting to see that God is telling the story of Salvation in "TYPE/ANTITYPE?"

In Exodus 19 the LORD told Moses,

> "Now therefore, if you will obey My voice indeed, and keep My Covenant, then you shall be a peculiar treasure unto Me above all people; for all the earth is Mine." Exodus 19:5.

It is basically the same thing that Peter wrote:

> "But you are a chosen generation, a royal priesthood, a holy nation, a peculiar people; that you should show forth the praises of Him who has called you out of darkness into His marvelous light." 1 Peter 2:9.

God was preparing the Israelites for what was about to happen in chapter 20… the giving of the Law; the 10 Commandments.

> "And the LORD said to Moses, "Go to the people and sanctify them today and tomorrow, and let them WASH THEIR CLOTHES, and be ready against the THIRD DAY:

for the THIRD DAY the LORD will come down in the sight of all the people upon Mount Sinai." Exodus 19:10-11.

This is a particularly important part of the journey. So, let us break it down one point at a time:

Wash Their Clothes

Washing their clothes was symbolic of washing away SINS...

"And now why do you wait? Arise, and be baptized, and WASH AWAY YOUR SINS, calling on the Name of the Lord." Acts 22:16.

"And from Jesus Christ, who is the faithful witness, and the first begotten of the dead, and the Prince of the kings of the earth. Unto Him that loved us and WASHED US FROM OUR SINS IN HIS OWN BLOOD and has made us kings and priests unto God and His Father; to Him be glory and dominion for ever and ever. Amen." Revelation 1:5-6

"For we ourselves also were sometimes foolish, disobedient, deceived, serving various lusts and pleasures, living in malice and envy, hateful, and hating one another. But after that the kindness of God our Savior toward man appeared, not by works of righteousness which we have done, but according to His Mercy He saved us, BY THE WASHING OF REGENERATION, and renewing of the Holy Ghost: which He shed on us abundantly through Jesus Christ our Savior." Titus 3:3-6.

I could go on and on, but that should be sufficient to show you how washing their clothes in the Old Testament pointed to a spiritual reality of regeneration in the life of the elect.

Now, On To The Third Day.

It is VERY, VERY IMPORTANT for the purpose of this writing, to understand the way that God sometimes looks at a DAY. To explain this especially important concept, we will start in the beginning...

> *"And the LORD God took the man and put him into the garden of Eden to dress it and to keep it. And the LORD God commanded the man, saying, "Of every tree of the garden you may freely eat but the tree of the knowledge of good and evil, you shall not eat of it: for IN THE DAY that you eat thereof you shall surely die." Genesis 2:15-17.*

We all know the story, right? Adam and Eve disobeyed God and were cast from the garden. But He said,

> *"IN THE DAY that you eat thereof you shall die."*

So, let me ask you: Did Adam and Eve die THAT DAY?

The answer is YES, but probably not for the reasons you may have been taught.

This passage of scripture has provided "scholars" and "commentators" difficulty forever because it is apparent that Adam and Eve went on to live long lives (in comparison to ours).

So, theologians have said that: "God was not speaking literally, Adam and Eve died SPIRITUALLY that day. He was speaking in a "Spiritual Context." I strongly disagree. Once again: The Bible will explain itself if you let it. The confusion arises because

"Theologians" (I still use that term loosely) do not understand how God perceives time.

> *"For a thousand years in your sight are as yesterday when it is past, and as a watch in the night." Psalm 90:4.*

> *"But beloved, BE NOT IGNORANT OF THIS ONE THING, that ONE DAY is with the LORD as a thousand years and A THOUSAND YEARS as one day." 2 Peter3:8.*

So, I will ask the question again: Did Adam and Eve die that day? The answer is YES.

> *Adam lived to be 930 years old. Genesis 5:5.*

Scripture does not say how long Eve lived but does record the life span of the person who lived longest upon the earth.

> *"And all the days of Methuselah were nine hundred sixty and nine years: and he died." Genesis 5:27.*

969 years is an exceptionally long time to live from our perspective but look at it from God's perspective. God originally created Man to live forever. To have access to the Tree of Life.

> 969 years is just short of 1000 years which God sees as 1 DAY.

So yes, they did die "THAT DAY." And, 969 years, or the 100 years of our lifespan are but a drop in the ocean of eternity.

James said it this way:

"For what is your life? It is just a vapor, that appears for a little time and then vanishes away." James 4:14b.

Let us follow Peter's advice and "be not ignorant" of the formula: 1 DAY = 1 THOUSAND YEARS, and 1 THOUSAND YEARS = 1 DAY. It is VERY IMPORTANT; that is why Peter placed such great emphasis on it.

Have you ever noticed that certain phrases and numbers are repeated over and over in the Scriptures?

Such as: the number 3... and especially, "the third day." Or the number 40? Or the number 7?

An entire book could be written (and has been) on the importance of numerology in Scripture, but for the purpose of this writing we will concentrate especially on the "3rd Day" and the "40 years."

Back To The Exodus:

We have seen how God told the Israelites to "wash their clothes" before approaching the Mountain of God and how that symbolized our "washing" of regeneration by the Holy Spirit. Just as God is teaching a spiritual reality through a temporal one, so also, He teaches time prophecies.

For example: He told the children of Israel to

"wash their clothes "today and tomorrow" "And BE READY against the THIRD DAY: for in the THIRD DAY the LORD will "COME DOWN" in the sight of all the people." Exodus 19:10-11.

Notice once again the timeline: Wash clothes for 2 days (2000 years) and IN (not after) the 3rd DAY the LORD will come down...

Jesus was crucified and risen in 31 AD and the "New Covenant" began, enabling us to wash our clothes in the blood of the Lamb for the next 2000 years (2 Days) when He will "come down" once again, IN the 3rd DAY.

> "For the Lord Himself shall DESCEND from heaven with a SHOUT, with the voice of the archangel, and with the TRUMPET of God: and the dead in Christ shall RISE first: Then we which are alive and remain shall be caught up together with them in the clouds to meet the Lord in the air; and so, shall we ever be with the Lord." 1 Thessalonians 4:16-17.

God is teaching us SPIRITUAL REALITIES through type/antitype.

When the children of Israel finally did enter the "promised land" the first city to conquer was Jericho. Notice HOW it was conquered:

> "And the seven priests shall bear before the ark seven trumpets of ram's horns: and the seventh day you shall compass the city seven times and the priests shall blow with the trumpets. And it shall come to pass that when they make a long blast with the ram's horn, and when you hear the SOUND OF THE TRUMPET, all the people shall SHOUT with a great SHOUT; and the wall of the city shall fall down flat, and the people SHALL ASCEND UP every man straight before him." "And it came to pass at the seventh time, when the priests blew with the TRUMPETS, Joshua said unto the people, "SHOUT;" For the LORD has given you the city." Joshua 6:4-5,16.

Once again, God is teaching SPIRITUAL REALITIES through type/antitype.

There are 2000 years (2 days) separating the creation of Adam from the birth of Abraham.

There are 2000 years (2 days) separating the birth of Abraham from the birth of Jesus.

There are 2000 years (2 days) separating the birth of Jesus to us today. (approx.).

2 + 2 + 2 = 6... For SIX days (6000 years) the priests blew the trumpet. But on the 7th DAY they made a LONG BLAST with the TRUMPET and made a SHOUT.

This is another way to recon the 2nd coming of Jesus... 6000 years of existence here on earth (6 Days) and then the 7th Day of rest... (Sabbath). We shall live and reign with Christ for what is called "The Millennial Reign" which is literally the 7th Day.

> "And I saw thrones, and they sat upon them, and judgment was given to them: and I saw the souls of them that were beheaded for the witness of Jesus, and for the Word of God, and which had not worshipped the beast, neither his image neither had received his mark upon their foreheads, or in their hands; AND THEY LIVED AND REIGNED WITH CHRIST A THOUSAND YEARS. But the rest of the dead lived not again until the thousand years were finished. This is the first resurrection. Blessed and holy is he that has part in the first resurrection: on such the second death has no power, but they shall be priests of God and of Christ AND SHALL REIGN WITH HIM A THOUSAND YEARS." (THE 7TH DAY). Revelation 20:4-6.

The children of Israel were promised a land "flowing with milk and honey": i.e. "The promised land." So, when the LORD led them to the Jordan River, which served as a border, the children of Israel sent spies into the land to check it out. Out of the 12 spies sent in, only 2, Joshua and Caleb, had faith that they would be able to overthrow the city. The other 10 spies said that there was NO WAY that they would be able to conquer the city even though God had told them that He would fight for them.

So, the LORD turned them around and led them through the wilderness for the next 40 years so that all that generation would perish in the desert and not enter in (except for Joshua and Caleb).

"But with whom was He grieved forty years? Was it not with them that had sinned, whose carcasses fell in the wilderness? And to whom He swore that they should not enter into His rest, but to them that believed not? So, we see that they could not enter in because of unbelief. Let us therefore fear lest a promise being left us of entering into His rest any of you should seem to come short of it. For unto us was the gospel preached, AS WELL AS UNTO THEM: but the Word preached did not profit them, not being mixed with faith in them that heard it. For we which have believed do enter into rest, as He said, "As I have sworn in My wrath if they shall enter into My rest:" although the works were finished from the foundation of the world. For He spoke in a certain place of the seventh day like this: "And God did rest the seventh day from all His works." And in this place again, "If they shall enter into My rest." Seeing therefore it remains that some must enter therein, and they to whom it was first preached entered not in because of unbelief: Again, He limits a certain day, saying in David (Psalms), "today, after so long a time; as it is said, today if you will hear His voice, harden not your hearts. For if Joshua had given them rest, then would he not afterward have spoken of another day? THERE REMAINS THEREFORE A REST TO THE PEOPLE OF GOD. For he that is entered into His rest, he also has ceased from his own works, as God did from His. Let us

labor therefore to enter into that rest, lest any man fall after the same example of unbelief." Hebrews 3:17 – 4:11.

Notice that the author of Hebrews says that the Gospel was preached to the children of Israel as well as to us... So, let me ask you, how was the gospel preached to them since they lived some 13 centuries before Christ?

Answer: In type.

God is so exacting in this method of teaching, that He would not let Moses enter the Promised Land with the rest of Israel. (Numbers 20:12). Because Moses messed up the type when he struck the Rock twice.

He is also so methodical and precise in the type/antitype presentation that the children of Israel had to first travel through the territory of Reuben, then into the territory of Gad, cross the Jordan and camp at Gilgal, and then on to Jericho.

Stay with me, why is all this important? Because: REUBEN means: "SEE YOU A SON"

GAD is pronounced: GAWD (with an "a" as in father). (God)

JORDAN means: to DESCEND.

Gilgal: the root word for Gilgal is GALGAL and is translated HEAVEN once at Psalms 77:18.

Jericho: means CITY OF THE MOON. Genesis 1:14 says the Sun and Moon are for SIGNS and seasons, and for days and years.

So, let us put the whole Exodus into context... from the day they left Egypt, to the day they entered the promised land and conquered Jericho.

The LAMB WAS SLAIN. Exodus 12. John 1:29.

Israel was protected by the BLOOD OF THE LAMB. 1st Passover.

Israel FOLLOWED GOD by a pillar of fire by night and cloud by day. Exodus 13:21-22.

Israel WAS BAPTIZED in the Red Sea. Exodus 14, 1 Corinthians 10:2.

Israel ATE BREAD FROM HEAVEN. Manna = MAN. Coriander = GOD. Exodus 16, John 6.

Israel DRANK FROM THE ROCK. Exodus 17. Numbers 20. 1 Corinthians 10:4.

Israel journeyed through and camped in the wilderness of SIN. Exodus 16:1, Numbers 33:11.

Israel journeyed through the wilderness 40 YEARS. Exodus 16:35. Numbers 14:33.

REUBEN/GAD GIVEN TERRITORY ON THE EAST SIDE OF JORDAN. Numbers 32. (SEE THE SON OF GOD).

Israel entered the PROMISED LAND after 40 YEARS. Joshua 4:19

Israel camped at GILGAL (HEAVEN) Joshua 4:19.

Israel is CIRCUMSIZED. Joshua 5:2,7.

Israel CONQUERED JERICHO WITH A TRUMPET AND A SHOUT. Joshua 6. 1 Thessalonians 4:16-17.

God is telling a story here!
1. To be delivered from bondage (to sin) we must accept the blood sacrifice of Jesus on the cross. 1 Corinthians 5:7.
2. We must follow God.
3. We are to be baptized. Acts 2:38.
4. We are to observe communion. John 6:56.
5. We must journey through this sinful world. 1 John 5:19.
6. We will not "crossover" to our promised land without SEEING the SON OF GOD. John 6:40.
7. We will be circumcised (heart) and changed. Deuteronomy 10:16. Romans 2:28-29. Ezekiel 36:26-28.

Jeremiah 31:31-35. 1 Corinthians 15:51-52.

We will be conquerors with Christ at the last Trumpet and Shout! Romans 8:37. 1 Thessalonians 4:16-17.

The only point that I skipped from the outline above is the part about Israel entering the promised land after 40 years... this was by design because it is the most important part of the Exodus narrative for us today. It is the key to understanding the time period allotted for the 2nd Coming of Jesus. Therefore, I wanted to dedicate more than just a few words to the subject.

The 40 Years Of Wilderness Wandering

There is no doubt that the 40 years of trials and tribulation that the children of Israel endured were meant to be an example to us today.

> *"Now all these things happened to them for "ensamples:" and they are written for our "admonition," upon whom the ends of the world are come." 1 Corinthians 10;11.*

We have already covered the meaning of "ensample," but it is worthy of revisiting. Ensample comes from the Greek word TUPOS and is the same word from which we get the English word "TYPE."

ADMONITION means a "mild rebuke or warning." And are written for us upon whom the ends of the world are come.

The children of Israel's release from bondage in Egypt closely resembles an important precept of Gods sovereignty and provision for His chosen people...

The Jubilee

God does not intend for His people to be slaves. However, we must work for a living because even in the New Testament it is written that if anyone refuses to work, he should not eat. 2 Thessalonians 3:10.

The Jubilee provided a "reset" of sorts to God's people. It also provided a reset for the land because every seven years the land was to rest from farming and on the fiftieth year it got a 2-year rest.

"Six years shall you sow your field, and then six years you shall prune your vineyard, and gather in the fruit thereof; but in the 7th year shall be a Sabbath of rest unto the land, a Sabbath for the LORD; you shall neither sow your field nor prune your vineyard. And you shall number seven sabbaths of years unto you, 7 times 7 years; And the space of the seven sabbaths of years shall be unto you 49 years. Then you shall cause the trumpet of the jubilee to sound on the 10th day of the 7th month, in the day of atonement you shall make the trumpet sound throughout all your land. And you shall hallow the 50th year and PROCLAIM LIBERTY throughout all the land unto all the inhabitants thereof; It shall be a jubilee unto you; And you shall return every man unto his possession, and you shall return every man unto his family. For it is a jubilee; It shall be holy to you; You shall eat the increase thereof out of the field. In the year of this jubilee, you shall return every man unto his possession. Leviticus 25:3-4, 8-10, 12-13.

Leviticus 25 (the whole chapter) gives instruction about the Jubilee, please take the time to read it for yourself and familiarize yourself with the concept that it is a release from bondage, or indentured servitude for God's people. It is also a Sabbath of rest, not only for the people but for the land as well.

Notice also, that the TRUMPET OF THE JUBILEE WAS TO SOUND ON THE 10TH DAY OF THE 7TH MONTH ON THE DAY OF ATONEMENT.

The Day Of Atonement

Trying to keep God's law is an impossible task, so the children of Israel were required to offer animal sacrifices to atone for their sins. Symbolically, as they came to the tabernacle and deposited their sins there day by day, a ritual cleansing of the holy place became a necessity and must occur once a year on the Day of Atonement. The priest would cast lots for 2 goats. One goat was to be sacrificed and the other was to be led into the wilderness far from camp and set free. The Priest would transfer the sins of Israel which had been deposited there to the goat and the "scapegoat" would be led to the wilderness.

This whole scenario was of course symbolic and was a "type" of the true scapegoat. There are 2 different camps on the theological significance of the scapegoat. First, that the scapegoat represents Satan, and the wilderness represents the bottomless pit. Revelation 20:2-3. Secondly, that the scapegoat represents Christ who took on the sins of the world on the cross. 1 Peter 2:24.

No matter which camp you are in, of a surety the lot that fell upon the goat that was to be sacrificed, was a type of Jesus Christ. Leviticus 16, Hebrews 9. If you read these 2 chapters in your Bible and ask the Holy Spirit to reveal truth to you, you will have a greater understanding of the sacrificial system instituted by God and the realities that it represented or pointed forward to.

The Day of Atonement, (Yom Kippur in Hebrew) was the Holiest Day of the Hebrew calendar and was the only day in which the Hebrews were commanded to "FAST and afflict their souls."

Leviticus 16:31, 23:27-28.

By the time Isaiah prophesied, the children of Israel had apostatized the observance of the Day of Atonement. By the time that Jesus began His Ministry, they had completely lost the theological significance and instead used the observance as an opportunity to show MEN how holy they were.

"Moreover, when you fast be not as the hypocrites, of a sad countenance; for they disfigure their faces that they may appear unto men to fast. Verily I say unto you, they have their reward." Matthew 6:16.

"Cry aloud, spare not, lift up your voice like a TRUMPET, and show My People their transgression and the house of Jacob their sins. Yet they seek Me daily, and delight to know My Ways, as a nation that did righteousness, and forsook not the ordinance of their God: they ask of Me the ordinances of justice; they take delight in approaching to God. Why have we fasted, say they, and you see not? Why have we afflicted our soul, and you take no knowledge? Behold, in the day of your fast you find pleasure, and exact all your labors. Behold, you fast for strife and debate, and to smite with the fist of wickedness: you shall not fast as you do this day, to make your voice to be heard on high. Is it such a fast that I have chosen? A day for a man to afflict his soul? Is it to bow down his head as a bulrush, and to spread sackcloth and ashes under him? Will you call this a fast, and an acceptable day to the LORD? Is not THIS THE FAST THAT I HAVE CHOSEN? To loosen the bands of wickedness, TO UNDO THE HEAVEY BURDENS, AND TO LET THE OPPRESSED GO FREE, AND THAT YOU BREAK EVERY YOKE? Is it not to deal your bread to the hungry, and that you bring the poor that

are cast out to your house? When you see the naked, that you cover him; and that you hide not yourself from your own flesh? Then shall your light break forth as the morning, and your health shall spring forth speedily; and your righteousness shall go before you; the glory of the Lord shall be your re-reward. Then shall you call, and the Lord shall answer; You shall cry, and He shall say, here I am. If you take away from you the yolk, the putting forth of the finger, and speaking vanity; and if you draw out your soul to the hungry, and satisfy the afflicted soul; then shall your light rise in obscurity, and your darkness be as the noonday; And the Lord shall guide you continually, and satisfy your soul in the drought, and make fat your bones; And you shall be like a watered garden, and like a spring of water, whose waters fail not. And they that shall be of you shall build the old waste places; You shall raise up the foundations of many generations; And you shall be called, the repairer of the breach, the restorer of paths to dwell in." Isaiah 58:1-12.

Notice that the Day of Atonement is inextricably linked to the JUBILEE. In other words: God says that the fast that He has chosen should point the person towards true righteousness: to undo heavy burdens, LET THE OPPRESSED GO FREE, and to break every YOKE... This is exactly what the Year of Jubilee was designed to do... and it is EXACTLY what Jesus does for us:

"Take My yoke upon you and learn of Me; for I am meek and lowly in heart; and you shall find rest unto your souls. For My yoke is easy, and My burden is light." Matthew 11:29-30.

"If the Son therefore shall make you free, you shall be free

indeed." John 8:36.

But instead of pointing Israel toward true righteousness, the ruling elite (Sanhedrin, Pharisees, Sadducees, Scribes) relegated the observances of God to "carnal observances."

> *"Now when these things were thus ordained, the priest went always into the first Tabernacle accomplishing the service of God. But into the second went the high priest alone once every year, not without blood, which he offered for himself and for the errors of the people; The Holy Ghost thus signifying, that the way into the holiest of all was not yet made manifest, while as the first Tabernacle was yet standing; which was a figure for the time then present, in which were offered both gifts and sacrifices, that could not make him that did the service perfect, as pertaining to the conscience; which stood only in meats and drinks and various washings and carnal ordinances, imposed on them until the time of reformation." Hebrews 9:6-10.*

Can you see the type/antitype of the Exodus being an escape, from bondage to sin?

Can you see the type/antitype of the wilderness wandering being our wilderness wandering in this world?

Can you see the type/antitype of the entrance of Israel into the promised land being our entrance into our promised land?

Now let us explore the connection of the Jubilee with Atonement a bit more so we can understand what the 40 years of wilderness wandering represents.

The word JUBILEE occurs 22 times in Scripture; and all except one occurrence it is the Hebrew word: YOWBEL; pronounced "yo-bale" and means: THE BLAST OF A HORN (from its continuous sound); specifically, THE SIGNAL OF THE SILVER TRUMPETS.

Do you see where this is leading?

The other occurrence on the word JUBILEE is the Hebrew word: TERUWAH; pronounced "Ter-oo-aw" and means: ACCLAMATION OF JOY OR A BATTLE-CRY; especially CLANGOR OF TRUMPETS, AS AN ALARM. This is also the same Hebrew word that is translated SHOUT in Joshua 6:5,20. (the "great shout").

So, the Jubilee, the Day of Atonement, the 2nd Coming of Christ, and the Exodus narrative are most definitely and inextricably linked and intertwined.

Therefore: What did the 40-year time period of the wilderness wandering represent?

Answer: The 40 Years Represented 40 Jubilees.

A JUBILEE IS 50 YEARS. 7 X 7 = 49 + 1 = 50. Leviticus 25:10.

40 X 50 = 2000. (One jubilee for every year of wilderness wandering).

The Exodus story starts with the Passover Lamb being sacrificed.

Jesus was crucified 31 AD... On the Passover.

31 + 2000 = 2031 AD.

This is just one more way that God has shown us the time allotted for Christ's return. But remember that that time will be cut short (Matthew 24:22) so that NO ONE knows the day or the hour.

"For the Lord Himself shall descend from Heaven with a SHOUT, with the voice of the archangel and with the TRUMPET of God: and the dead in Christ shall rise first;

Then we which are alive and remain shall be caught up to-gether with them in the clouds to meet the Lord in the air; and so, shall we ever be with the Lord. Wherefore comfort one another with these words." 1 Thessalonians 4:16-18.

Jesus Is Coming!!!!....... Soon.

CHAPTER 15

THE WEDDING

God is the one who ordained the institution of marriage. He said,

> *"It is not good that man should be alone. I will make a helper for him." Genesis 2:18.*

So God took a rib from Adam and made a woman, Eve.

> *"Therefore, shall a man leave his father and his mother, and shall cleave unto his wife: and they shall be one flesh." Genesis 2:24.*

The institution of marriage, or as some call it: Holy matrimony, is meant to be a union between man and woman for life. Jesus explained it this way when the Pharisee said:

> *"Is it lawful for a man to put away (divorce) his wife for every cause?" And He answered, "Have you not read that He which made them at the beginning made them male and female, and said, for this cause shall a man leave father and mother and shall cleave to his wife: and they two shall be one flesh? Wherefore, they are no more two,*

but one flesh. What therefore God has joined together, let not man separate." They said to Him, "Why did Moses then command to give a writing of divorcement, and to put her away?" He said to them, "Moses, because of the hardness of your hearts allowed you to put away your wives: but from the beginning it was not so." And I say to you, "Whosoever shall put away his wife, EXCEPT IT BE FOR FORNICATION, and SHALL MARRY ANOTHER, commits adultery: and whosoever marries her which is put away does also commit adultery." Matthew 19:3-9.

A couple of points should be made here:

First, the Hebrew word translated CLEAVE is DABAQ, pronounced daw-bak', and means: to impinge, i.e., cling or adhere; figuratively to catch by pursuit.

Isn't that what God does? "Pursue" us?

"We love Him, because He first loved us." 1 John 4:19.

-"No man can come to Me, except the Father which has sent Me DRAW him: and I will raise him up at the last day." John 6:44.

The Greek word translated DRAW is: HELKUO, pronounced: hel-koo'-o and means: TO DRAG. (Literally or figuratively).

Secondly, why is fornication the exception to the prohibition against divorce?

Answer: because God looks at marriage as a "union" that is made between a man and woman.

In other words: we say the marriage is "consummated" when the couple has sex on their wedding night. The two have joined themselves together, literally, and become one flesh. If either one of them steps outside the bounds of this "union" then in Gods eyes they are joining themselves to another and this act constitutes "divorce."

Spiritually, marriage is the same concept. The LORD accused Israel of WHORING around repeatedly because they sought after the "gods" of surrounding peoples... So much so, that He divorced Israel. (But only because she had played the harlot).

"The LORD said unto me in the days of Josiah the king, "Have you seen that which backsliding Israel has done? She is gone up upon every high mountain and under every green tree, and there has played the HARLOT." And I said after she had done all these things, "Turn back to Me." But she returned not. And her treacherous sister Judah saw it. And I saw, when for all the causes whereby backsliding Israel committed adultery, I had put her away, and given her a bill of DIVORCE; yet her treacherous sister Judah feared not but went and played the harlot also. And it came to pass through the lightness of her whoredom, that she defiled the land, and committed adultery with stones and with stocks (wood). And yet for all this, her treacherous sister Judah has not turned to Me with her whole heart, but feignedly, says the LORD. And the LORD said to me, "The backsliding Israel has justified herself more than treacherous Judah. Go and proclaim these words toward the north, and say, "Return, you backsliding Israel, says the LORD; and I will not cause My anger to fall upon you: for I am merciful, says the LORD, and I will not keep anger forever. Only acknowledge your iniquity, that you have transgressed against the LORD your God, and have scattered your ways to the strangers under every green tree, and you have not obeyed My voice, says the LORD. Turn, O backsliding children says the LORD; for I AM MARRIED TO YOU; and I will take you one of a city, and two of a family, and I will bring you to

Zion: and I will give you pastors according to My Heart, which shall feed you with knowledge and understanding." Jeremiah 3:6-15.

"Thus says the LORD, "Where is the bill of your mother's divorcement, whom I have put away? Or, which of My creditors is it to whom I have sold you? Behold, for YOUR INIQUITIES have you SOLD YOURSELVES and for YOUR TRANGRESSIONS is your mother put away." Isaiah 50:1.

God is longsuffering and kind, but He is also the Righteous Judge and so many more things including but not limited to: Provider, Sustainer, Healer, Shepard, and our Husband. He sent prophets to His people to warn them of their backsliding ways, but they misused and killed them. As a result, Israel was carried away into captivity in 722 BCE by the Assyrians.

Her sister Judah saw what happened to Israel and refused to repent as well and were carried away captive by the Babylonians in 586 and 597 BCE. (2 deportations).

The good news is that the LORD does not stay angry forever. In the book of Hosea, God instructs Hosea to marry a prostitute, Gomer...

"So, he went and took Gomer the daughter of Diblaim; which conceived and bare him a son. And the LORD said to him, "Call his name Jezreel; for yet a little while, and I will avenge the blood of Jezreel upon the house of Jehu and will cause to cease the kingdom of the house of Israel. And it shall come to pass at that day, that I will break the bow of Israel in the valley of Jezreel. And she conceived again and bare a daughter. And God said unto him, "Call her name Loruhamah; for I will no longer have mercy upon the house of Israel; but I will utterly take them

away. But I will have mercy upon the house of Judah, and will save them by the LORD their God, and will not save them by bow, nor by sword, nor by battle, by horses, nor by horsemen. Now when she had weaned Loruhamah she conceived and bare a son. Then said God, "Call his name Loammi: for you are not My people, and I will not be your God." Hosea 1:3-9.

It sounds serious does it not? Thank God He is forgiving! We will continue.

"Yet the number of the children of Israel shall be as the sand of the sea which cannot be measured nor numbered: and it shall come to pass that in the place where it was said unto them, "You are not My people" there it shall be said unto them, "You are the sons of the living God." Then shall the children of Judah and the children of Israel be gathered together, and appoint themselves one head, and they shall come up out of the land; for great shall be the day of Jezreel." Hosea 1:10-11.

"And I will betroth you unto Me forever; yes, I will betroth you unto Me in righteousness, and in judgment, and in lovingkindness, and in mercies. I will even betroth you unto Me in faithfulness: and you shall know the LORD." Hosea 2:19-20.

It is always good to see a story that starts out so shaky ends well.

I hope that you see that God Almighty has a "love affair" with Israel. (For lack of a better term).

I also hope you understand that if you are "saved" or part of the "elect" or "chosen" or "remnant" whatever term you want to use, that you are part of ISRAEL.

"Has God cast away His people? God forbid... God has not cast away His people which He foreknew." Romans 11:1a,2a.

"And so, all Israel shall be saved; as it is written: There shall come out of Sion the Deliverer and shall turn away ungodliness from Jacob." Romans 11:26

"For he is not a Jew which is one outwardly; neither is that circumcision which is outward in the flesh: But he is a Jew which is one INWARDLY: and circumcision is that of THE HEART, in the SPIRIT, and not in the letter; whose praise is not of men, but of God." Romans 2:28-29.

If you are a partaker of the New Covenant, you are SPIRITUALLY a Jew. Grafted into Israel. And you are "betrothed" to the LORD. Betrothed means: engaged for matrimony.

Speaking of the church at Corinth Paul said,

"For I am jealous over you with godly jealousy: for I have ESPOUSED you to one Husband, that I may present you as a CHASTE VIRGIN to Christ." 2 Corinthians 11:2.

The Marriage Of The Lamb

"The kingdom of heaven is like a certain king which made a marriage for his son. And sent forth his servants to call them that were invited to the wedding: and they

would not come. Again, he sent forth other servants, saying, "Tell them which are invited, Behold, I have prepared my dinner: my oxen and my fatlings are killed, and all things are ready: Come to the marriage." But they made light of it, and went their ways one to his farm, another to his merchandise: And the remnant took his servants and treated them spitefully and killed them. But when the king heard of this, he was mad: and he sent forth his armies and destroyed those murderers and burned their city. Then he said to his servants, "The wedding is ready but they which were invited are not worthy. Therefore, go into the highways, and as many as you shall find, invite to the marriage. So those servants went out into the highways and gathered together as many as they could find, both bad and good: and the wedding was furnished with guests. And when the king came in to see the guests, he saw there a man which had not on a wedding garment: and he said to him, "Friend how do you come in here not having a wedding garment?" And he was speechless. Then the king said to the servants, "Bind him hand and foot and take him away and cast him into outer darkness; there shall be weeping and gnashing of teeth. For many are called, but few are chosen." Matthew 22:2-14.

The Wedding Garment Is Important.

But what does it represent?

"Let us be glad and rejoice and give honor to Him: for the marriage of the Lamb has come and His wife has made herself ready. And to her was granted that she should be arrayed in FINE LINEN, clean and white: for THE FINE LINEN IS THE RIGHTEOUSNESS OF SAINTS. And He said to me, "Write, "Blessed are they which are called to the

marriage supper of the Lamb." And He said to me, "These are the true sayings of God." Revelation 19:7-9.

I might be in trouble if MY RIGHTEOUSNESS determines the condition of my wedding garments!

"After this I beheld, and lo, a great multitude, which no man could number of all nations, and kindreds, and people, and tongues, stood before the throne, and before the Lamb, clothed with WHITE ROBES, and palms in their hands; and cried with a loud voice, saying, "Salvation to our God which sits upon the throne, and unto the Lamb." And all the angels stood round about the throne, and about the elders and the four beasts, and fell before the throne on their faces, and worshipped God, saying, "Amen: Blessing, and glory, and wisdom, and thanksgiving, and honor, and power and might, be unto our God forever and ever. Amen." And one of the elders answered, saying to me, "What are these which are dressed in white robes? And from where did they come?" And I said to Him, "Sir, you know." And he said to me, "These are they which came out of great tribulation, and have WASHED THEIR ROBES, and made them white in THE BLOOD OF THE LAMB." Revelation 7:9-14.

I feel much better now! It is not MY righteousness, but the righteousness of the Lamb, Jesus Christ. That is a relief! Of course, this passage is speaking symbolically to a spiritual principle. In this temporal world we know that blood stains clothes and makes them darker not white. But spiritually speaking, if we are covered in the blood of the Lamb, we are protected just like the Israelites at the first Passover.

Remember, the Bible is a spiritual book, written by holy men of God who were moved by the Holy Spirit. (2 Peter 1:21) Keep the spiritual aspects and the type/antitype method of exegesis in mind as we continue.

Marriage In Cana Of Galilee

The Gospel of John is rich in theological meaning. His gospel opens with:

> "In the beginning,"

just like Genesis only John adds deep insights to the narrative proclaiming Jesus to be the Word of God.

> "In Him was life; and the life was the light of men." John 1:4.

Very deep when you think about it. John is speaking metaphorically, and the implications have great spiritual significance.

After John's introduction, the body of his discourse turns to the baptism of Jesus. (John 1:25-34). This act of baptism and the Holy Ghost descending upon Jesus began His 3 ½ year ministry.

It also began His invitation to the "wedding" with the words: "Follow Me." Two of John the Baptists' disciples were first, one of the two was Andrew, Simon Peter's brother, who found Simon and told him that he had met the Messiah. Peter then went to Jesus. The next was Philip and then Nathaniel.

Keep in mind the parable of the kingdom of Heaven that started this chapter, that parable ended with: "For many are called, but few are chosen." The disciples are definitely called (to the wedding) and chosen (to remain).

> *"And the THIRD DAY there was a marriage in Cana of*
> *Galilee; and the mother of Jesus was there: and both Jesus*
> *was CALLED, and HIS DISCIPLES, to the MARRIAGE."*
> *John 2:1-2.*

Let us stop right here and analyze the theological significance.

Why did the Holy Spirit (through John) record the "third day?" Wouldn't the text be just as clear by saying, "And there was a marriage in Cana of Galilee?" No, it would not. Why not? You may ask.

Because John is counting down the days for a reason. John's introduction from chapter 1, verse 1, to verse 28, is day 1.

Verse 29 begins with the words: "The next day." Which is the beginning of day 2. Day 2 continues to verse 34.

Day 3 begins with the words: "Again the next day," in verse 35 and ends in verse 42.

Day 4 begins with the words: "The day following," and continues to the end of chapter 1 verse 51... and that brings us to:

"And the third day," of chapter 2 verse 1.

Reflect for just a moment... Didn't John, led by the Holy Spirit, begin his gospel with the words:

> *"In the beginning,"*

just like the book of Genesis? Also, doesn't John count down the days just as in Genesis? (See: Genesis 1: 5,8,13,19,23,31.) (John 1: 29,35,43,).

So, I will ask the question once again, WHY did the Holy Spirit record "THE THIRD DAY?"

Because it has great theological significance for us.
That is why.

How so? You may ask.

4 days were recorded in chapter one. The "third day" from the four days recorded in chapter one brings us to the 7th Day.

The 7th day begins chapter 2 of John's gospel.

The 7th day begins chapter 2 of Genesis as well.

Let us explore the similarities between Genesis 2 and John 2.

Genesis 2 speaks of the Sabbath of rest. It is a sanctified, set apart day, the 7th day. It also speaks of the creation of Adam and Eve and their job of tending the garden which contained the TREE OF LIFE. Genesis 2 speaks of what mankind LOST due to the "fall" of mankind.

John 2 speaks of a "Wedding" on the 7th Day.

It is the "wedding" of the Lamb that RESTORES the effects of the "fall."

It is the "Wedding" of the Lamb that restores the "Way" back to the tree of life. (Revelation 19:7, 22: 2).

The Third Day

The synoptic gospels record that Jesus took the cup of wine at the "Last Supper" and gave it to His disciples to drink and then added these words:

> "I will drink no more of the fruit of the vine (wine) until that day that I drink it new in the kingdom of God." Matthew 26:29, Mark 14:25, Luke 22:18.

Jesus is going to wait until the Marriage Supper of the Lamb to drink wine with us in the Kingdom of God! Hallelujah! Revelation 19:9.

And when will this be?

And why did John record days one through four in his gospel (ch.1) and not record days 5 & 6?

Because, if he had recorded the events of days 5 & 6, he would have started Chapter 2 with

"And the next day"

... or something similar and would NOT have been able to attach the words

"And the THIRD DAY"

to the marriage and the wine.

Remember the formula: 1 Day = 1 Thousand Years and 1 Thousand Years = 1 Day.

Jesus was crucified and risen in 31 AD.

2 Days = 2000 Years.

31 AD + 2000 Years = 2031 AD.

2031 AD will begin the "third day."

This is just one more way in which God has given us the time period allotted to "the time of the end."

Jesus Is Coming For His Saints Who Have Washed Their Robes In The Blood Of The Lamb.

CHAPTER 16

THE TEMPLE PART 2

God has created many marvelous things and has revealed some of His creation to us. Increasingly, we can explore the vastness of the cosmos with space-based telescopes and see for ourselves the majesty of God's creation.

On rare occasions, the LORD gives someone a vision of heaven or what awaits us in the New Jerusalem.

The apostle John was one such lucky soul, as was Moses.

John wrote:

> "And the Temple of God was opened in heaven, and there was seen in His Temple the ark of His testament: and there were lightnings, and voices, and thundering's, and an earthquake, and great hail." Revelation 11:19.

Moses wrote:

> "And let them make Me a sanctuary; that I may dwell among them. According to all that I show you, after the pattern of the tabernacle, and the pattern of all the instruments thereof, even so shall you make it. And look that you make them after their pattern, which was showed to you in the Mount." Exodus 25:8-9,40.

The earthly Temple and Tabernacle were but re-creations of the "True Tabernacle" in Heaven. As the LORD has shown us repeatedly, the temporal points us to a greater spiritual reality. The Temple is no different.

"Now of the things which we have spoken this is the sum: We have such a High Priest, who is set on the right hand of the throne of the Majesty in the heavens; a minister of the sanctuary, and of the TRUE TABERNACLE, which the Lord pitched, and not man. For every high priest is ordained to offer gifts and sacrifices: wherefore it is of necessity that this Man have somewhat also to offer. For if He were on earth, He should not be a priest, seeing that there are priests that offer gifts according to the law: Who serve unto the EXAMPLE AND SHADOW OF HEAVENLY THINGS, as Moses was admonished of God when he was about to make the Tabernacle: for, See, He said, that you make all things according to the pattern shown to you in the mount. But now He has obtained a more excellent ministry, by how much also He is the mediator of a better covenant, which was established upon better promises. For if that first covenant had been faultless, then should no place have been sought for the second. For finding fault with them, He said, "Behold, the days come says the LORD, when I will make a New Covenant with the house of Israel and with the house of Judah: Not according to the covenant that I made with their fathers in the day when I took them by the hand to lead them out of the land of Egypt; because they continued not in My Covenant, and I regarded them not, says the LORD. For this is the covenant that I will make with the house of Israel after those days, Says the LORD; I will put My laws into their mind, and write them in their hearts: and I will be to them a God and they shall be to Me a people: and they shall not teach every man his neighbor , and every man his brother,

saying, "Know the LORD:" For all shall know Me, from the least to the greatest. For I will be merciful to their unrighteousness, and their sins and their iniquities will I remember no more. In that He says, A New Covenant, He has made the first old. Now that which decays and waxes old is ready to vanish away." Hebrews 8.

The earthly Tabernacle and Temple were representations of what is in Heaven. The furnishings of the Temple were designed to point us to spiritual realities such as: The table of Show-bread... or as it is sometimes called: Bread of the Presence. The bread was to be continually in the Holy place, the first compartment of the Temple.

Another is the 7-branch candlestick, the Menorah. The Menorah and the Showbread were representations of the Spiritual reality that we need Jesus to approach the Father in the most Holy Place, the Holy of Holies.

"I AM the Bread of Life." John 6:48.

"I AM come a light into the world, that whosoever believes in Me should not abide in darkness." John 12:46.

The altar of incense is where the priest would burn incense. Exodus 30.

The incense ascending is the vehicle for the prayers of the saints.

"And another angel came and stood at the altar, having a golden censer; and there was given to him much incense that he should offer it with the prayers of all saints upon the golden altar which was before the throne. And the smoke of the incense, which came with the prayers of the

saints, ascended up before God out of the angel's hand."
Revelation 8:3-4.

"And when He had taken the book, the four beasts and
twenty-four elders fell down before the Lamb, having
every one of them harps and golden vials full of odors,
which are the prayers of saints." Revelation 5:8.

I hope that you are beginning to see that the LORD teaches spiritual realities through the temporal furnishings of the Tabernacle/Temple. The purpose of this writing is to show you just how short the time period allotted for this existence is. It is not to explain every purpose of the furnishings... but some knowledge is required to be able to understand the Spiritual significance of the Temple and what it represents.

When God divorced Israel and sent them into captivity, and then sent her sister Judah into captivity, the Temple in Jerusalem was destroyed. This was the destruction of the 1st Temple commonly referred to as "Solomon's Temple."

After Judah had served her time in captivity (70 years), she was released to come home and rebuild the Temple under the leadership of Ezra and Nehemiah.

This Temple is referred to as the 2nd Temple and continued until it was defiled by Antiochus IV Epiphanes who set up the "abomination that makes desolate" (Daniel 11:31) on the altar of sacrifice. The Maccabees were able to repurify the Temple 3 years later and reinstate Temple worship.

Herod the Great thought that a good way to ingratiate himself to the Jews would be to dismantle the Temple and replace it with a grander design. This began in 20-19 BCE... This Temple remained until 70 CE when Rome destroyed the Temple under Titus.

The death and resurrection of Jesus in 31 CE ushered in a "New and Living Way." A physical Temple containing the ark of the covenant which contained the 2 tables of stone, the 10 commandments, was no longer required under the "New Covenant."

> *"For this is the covenant that I will make with the house of Israel; after those days, says the LORD, I will put My law in their inward parts, and write it in their hearts; and will be their God and they shall be My people." Jeremiah 31:33, Ezekiel 36:26-27, Hebrews 8:10, 10:16-17.*

The Temple, the 2 tables of stone, the law, the animal sacrifices, the drink offerings, sin offerings and most everything associated with the Temple was to point the Israelites to a much greater Spiritual Reality. (And us too).

With the law now written in our hearts, and with the help of the in-dwelling Spirit of God, believers have become the "Temple" of the "Christian era."

> *"Do not be unequally yoked together with unbelievers: for what fellowship has righteousness with unrighteousness? And what concord has Christ with Belial? Or what part has he that believes with an Infidel? And what agreement has the TEMPLE OF GOD with idols? FOR YOU ARE THE TEMPLE OF THE LIVING GOD; as God has said, "I will dwell in them, and walk in them; and I will be their God and they shall be My people." 2 Corinthians 6:14-16.*

> *"What? Don't you know that your body is the TEMPLE of the HOLY GHOST which is in you, which you have of God, and you are not your own?" 1 Corinthians 6:19.*

"Don't you know that you are the TEMPLE OF GOD, and that the Spirit of God dwells in you?" 1 Corinthians 3:16.

So, let us reflect for a moment.

The Tabernacle was where God met with Moses and Aaron in the wilderness.

The Temple is where God met with the Israelites once they entered the promised land.

Just before the death and resurrection of Jesus He told the Jews,

"Behold, your house (Temple) is left unto you desolate." Matthew 23:38.

He said this to them because He knew His time had come to lay down His life and usher in a New Age.

The Temple is now being built Spiritually, with Christ as the Chief Corner Stone, unto a "Spiritual House" a Holy Priesthood, to offer up Spiritual sacrifices, acceptable to God by Jesus Christ. 1 Peter 2:5.

We are the "Lively Stones" of this Spiritual Temple. 1 Peter 2:5.

So, if God is building this "SPIRITUAL TEMPLE" currently, then what happens to the Temple in Heaven once Jesus returns to get His Bride/Temple?

In other words, will there be 2 Temples in Heaven once we get there?

"And I saw a new heaven and a new earth: for the first heaven and the first earth were passed away; and there was no more sea. And I John saw the holy city, new Jerusalem, coming down from God out of heaven, prepared as a bride adorned for her husband. And I heard a great

> *voice out of heaven saying, "BEHOLD, THE TABERNACLE OF GOD IS WITH MEN, and He will dwell with them, and they shall be His people, and God Himself shall be with them, and be their God." Revelation 21:1-3.*

> *"And I saw NO TEMPLE THEREIN: for the LORD God Almighty and the Lamb are the Temple of it." Revelation 21:22.*

The answer to the question is NO. There will not be 2 Temples in the New Jerusalem. Everything will have been fulfilled.

So, consider this: Jesus will come sometime before 2031 to get His church/bride/temple (this will comprise 2 days, or 2000 years). Then the millennial reign, (this will add 1 more day or 1000 years) and then the New Jerusalem descends from Heaven as a bride adorned for her husband. So, from the time that Jesus was crucified until the "Spiritual Temple" is planted on the NEW Earth in the NEW Jerusalem it constitutes 3000 years or 3 DAYS.

Jesus said:

> *"Destroy this Temple and in 3 days I will raise it up." John 2:19.*

It is apparent that Jesus was talking of His body because Scripture makes it clear in verse 21.

But could He have also been talking about a deeper, Spiritual meaning? If so, it is one more way to recon the time allotted for this dispensation.

Jesus Is The Chief Cornerstone.

CHAPTER 17

THE FEASTS OF THE LORD

T he Feasts of the LORD were instituted after the Exodus from Egypt during the wilderness wandering.

There are 7 special "high day" Sabbaths associated with the Feasts and Festivals of the LORD. And, of course, every week there is a weekly Sabbath which begins at sundown Friday and continues to sundown Saturday.

The first of the Feasts is Passover. As we have already learned in previous chapters, the Passover is always a Preparation Day. It is also always associated with a full moon. The first month of the Hebrew Calendar is reckoned from the very first sliver of a New Moon which appears extremely low on the horizon at sundown in the Western sky. And, since the wave sheaf had to be presented during the Feast of Unleavened Bread, there also had to be standing grain in the field which was reaching maturity.

This first New Moon of the year was especially important to get right because the entire years calendar and the festivals and observances were counted from this New Year's Day.

Once the correct New Moon is observed, the count begins. Passover is on the 14th day of this first month which is called either Abib (which means "green ears") or Nisan and corresponds to our calendar as March/April. As mentioned in a previous chapter, God's method of dividing the year in the Springtime when trees are budding and coming back to life and when plants are putting forth green leaves makes much more sense than the way we have been taught to divide the year, in the dead of winter.

The Passover ushers in the Feast of Unleavened Bread which begins the next day, on the 15th of Abib, and continues for 7 days and ends on the 21st of Abib. The 1st High Day Sabbath of the year is the first day of the feast (15th) and the 2nd High Day is the 21st seven days later.

During the Feast of Unleavened Bread, the Israelites were required to have already cleaned all the leavening agents (yeast, fermented dough, etc.) from their dwellings so that nothing remained in their homes during the Feast that might be used to cause dough to ferment. It is this "putting away" of something that is seemingly small and insignificant, but which has great effect; that is spoken of in the New Testament.

"A little leaven leavens the whole lump." Galatians 5:9.

"Your glorying is not good. Don't you know that a little leaven leavens the whole lump? Purge out therefore the old leaven, that you may be a new lump, as you are unleavened. For even Christ our Passover is sacrificed for us: Therefore, let us keep the feast, not with old leaven, neither with the leaven of malice and wickedness; but with the unleavened bread of sincerity and truth." 1 Corinthians 5:6-8.

Once again, we see that the LORD teaches in type/antitype. The "Leaven" that Christians are to put away or "purge" from our lives include malice and wickedness (sin).

God is telling a story with His feast days. When we accept the sacrifice of Jesus and make Him the Lord of our lives and are covered in the blood (Passover) we are to put away sinful things to live an "unleavened" existence through the process of sanctification. We are not to be "lukewarm" but sincere and follow the path of truth.

> *"God is Spirit, and they that worship Him must worship Him in SPIRIT and in TRUTH." John 4:24.*

The Passover and the Feast of Unleavened Bread comprise 8 days. It is interesting to note that the LORD'S calendar begins and ends with 8-day observances. (The Passover and Unleavened Bread being the first and the Feast of Tabernacles being the last.) Since the Passover and the Feast of Unleavened Bread together consist of 8 days, there is always a weekly Sabbath contained therein. It is from the Sunday following this weekly Sabbath during the Feast of Unleavened Bread that the count begins for the Feast of Weeks (Pentecost) which is next on the Feast Day calendar.

> *"And you shall count unto you from the morrow after the Sabbath, from the day that you brought the sheaf of the wave offering: seven Sabbaths shall be complete: Even until the day after the seventh Sabbath shall you number fifty days; and you shall offer a new meat offering unto the LORD." Leviticus 23:15-16.*

Pentecost is 7 X 7 = 49 + 1 = 50.

Jubilee is 7 X 7 = 49 + 1 = 50.

Hmmmmmmmmmmm. Remarkably interesting.

We have already seen the implications that the Jubilee holds for reckoning the return of Jesus, so what implication does the count to Pentecost hold?

Pentecost is inextricably linked to the outpouring of the Holy Spirit in Acts 2 which occurred on the day of Pentecost.

Forget what you may have been taught by misguided Pastors or teachers for a moment concerning the Giving of the Holy Spirit. I say this because several years ago, I was speaking in a congregation and teaching about the "down payment" or "earnest" of the Holy Spirit which we have been given as believers. One of the church elders stood up and told the congregation to ignore what I was saying and then he said, "We already have all of the Holy Spirit that we are ever going to receive!"

> Well, this was not the first or the last time that I was called down for teaching concepts that were apparently above the hearers' comprehension.

Remember Paul said to the church at Corinth:

> *"I have fed you with milk, and not with meat because you are not able to bear it, and you are still not able." 1 Corinthians 3:2.*

So, if you have been taught the erroneous concept that you already have the gift of the Holy Spirit in its entirety please put those thoughts aside and keep an open mind.

If you owned a truck and had put a "FOR SALE" sign on it, and I was driving down the road and was interested in buying the truck, but did not have the entire sale price, I might ask you to take what money that I had at the time to HOLD THE TRUCK until I could return with the rest of the purchase price. The money that I would leave you until I returned is called EARNEST money. It means that I am SERIOUS about the transaction.

> *"Now He which establishes us with you in Christ and has anointed us is God, who has also sealed us and given the EARNEST of THE SPIRIT in our hearts." 2 Corinthians 1:21-22.*

"Now He that has wrought us for the selfsame thing is God, who also has given unto us the EARNEST of the SPIRIT." 2 Corinthians 5:5.

"You were sealed with that Holy Spirit of promise which is the EARNEST of our inheritance until the redemption of the purchased possession, unto the praise of His glory." Ephesians 1:13b-14.

The Greek word translated "earnest" only appears in the 3 examples above and is the word: arrhabon, and means a PLEDGE, i.e., part of the purchase-money or property given in advance as "security" for the rest.

Point made, let us move on.

Former And Latter Rain

Children nowadays think that food comes from a market. Many have been raised in the cities and have no concept of agricultural processes of planting, waiting for the rain to make crops grow, and harvest time. It has not always been so. Invariably there have been markets, but to be oblivious to the pastoral and agricultural way of life I think is a relatively new design.

God taught many of His object lessons using husbandry and horticulture which most people of the time of Jesus would understand.

One such object lesson was how He would come to us as the "former rain" and the "latter rain."

Think about it, springtime is a renewal of life and plants need rain which the LORD provides for the plants to take root and grow. And then the summertime comes when there is not as much rain. And then in the fall, the rain returns. This is the framework God used to tell us how He was to pour out His Spirit.

"Be glad then, you children of Zion, and rejoice in the LORD your God: for He has given you the FORMER RAIN moderately and He will cause to COME DOWN for you the rain, the FORMER RAIN and the LATTER RAIN in the first month. And the floors shall be full of wheat, and the vats shall overflow with wine and oil. And I will restore to you the years that the locust has eaten, the cankerworm, and the caterpillar and the palmerworm, My great army which I sent among you. And you shall eat in plenty and be satisfied and praise the name of the LORD your God, that has dealt wondrously with you: and My people shall never be ashamed. And you shall know that I AM in the midst of Israel, and that I AM the LORD your God, and none else; and My people shall never be ashamed. And it shall come to pass afterward, that I will pour out My Spirit upon all flesh: and your sons and your daughters shall prophesy, your old men shall dream dreams, your young men shall see visions: And, upon the servants and upon the handmaids in those days will I POUR OUT MY SPIRIT." Joel 2:23-29.

We know from Acts chapter 2 that this prophecy from the book of Joel was partially fulfilled with the "pouring out" of the Spirit at Pentecost 31 AD. This was the "former rain." See: Acts 2:16-21.

Jesus said that the kingdom of God was like the wheat harvest which we have already covered in an earlier chapter.

The former rain and latter rain which represents the pouring out of God's Spirit has an "appointed time" just as many other things do. Speaking of backsliding Israel, He said:

"Neither say they in their heart "Let us now fear the LORD our God, that gives rain, both the former and the latter, IN HIS SEASON; He reserves unto us THE APPOINTED WEEKS OF THE HARVEST." Jeremiah 5:24.

The point here is God has appointed a time for the outpouring of the "latter rain," just as the "former rain" was poured out at Pentecost.

I want you to pause and think about this for a moment: In the wintertime, trees go into hibernation, (except evergreens) crops die out, grass turns brown, and basically the world dies. But in springtime, everything springs back to life and the rains come and then spring turns to summer and there is a long hot summertime. But afterwards, the rains return and harvesttime is upon us once again.

Now think back in history. The former rain was poured out at Pentecost in 31 AD and continued to "rain" until the newly formed church was established with firm roots.

Then came the long hot summer of the "Middle Ages." During this "summertime" there was not much advancement in the arts, religion, or cultural pursuits. Illness was a problem with plagues and dysentery and tuberculosis etc.

But then came the "latter rains." A new day was dawning with what has been labeled the "Early Modern Era." In Europe it was called the "Renaissance," in the English colonies the revival or "coming back to life" was called the "Great Awakening." In Europe, this is when the Protestant Reformation gained traction and bloomed.

We are living in this time of "latter rain," and all we must do is ask and the Lord (and accept Jesus as our Savior of course) and He will give us His Spirit.

"Ask you of the LORD rain in the time of the latter rain; so, the LORD shall make bright clouds, and give them showers of rain, to EVERYONE grass in the field." Zechariah 10:1.

Being able to look back on history and see that we are in the times of the latter rain is paramount to understanding the time in which we find ourselves. Knowing that the harvest is rapidly approaching and time as we know it is ending, we wait patiently.

"Be patient therefore brethren, unto the coming of the Lord. Behold, the husbandman waits for the precious fruit of the earth and has long patience for it, until He receive THE EARLY AND LATTER RAIN." James 5:7.

Jesus Is The Husbandman. We Are The Fruit.

When Jesus returns to "harvest" the fruit, or "wheat" or whatever analogy you prefer, we will receive the REST of the PURCHASE PRICE… (holy spirit).

"You were sealed with the Holy Spirit of promise, which is the "Earnest" of our inheritance until the redemption of the purchased possession, unto the praise of His glory." Ephesians 1:13b-14.

"Behold I show you a mystery: We shall not all sleep, but we shall all be changed. In a moment, in the twinkling of an eye, at the last trumpet: for the trumpet shall sound, and the dead shall be raised incorruptible, and we shall be

changed." 1 Corinthians 15:51-52.

At the last trumpet we will receive the rest of the purchase price.

Back To The Feast Days:

After Pentecost, which is the 3ʳᵈ High Day Sabbath of the year, comes the Feast of Trumpets which occurs on the 1ˢᵗ day of the 7ᵗʰ month, which is called Tishri, and corresponds to our September / October. This is also a High Day Sabbath... the 4ᵗʰ of the Year. There is to be a blowing of the trumpets or Shofar (ram's horn) and no work is to be done.

The 10ᵗʰ day of this 7ᵗʰ month is the most Holy day of the year to post-exilic Israelites and is the 5ᵗʰ High Day Sabbath of the year, the Day of Atonement. No work is to be done and it is a day of afflicting one's soul (fasting) and reflecting on the solemnity of the event.

This day of course pointed forward to the Atoning Sacrifice of Jesus on the Cross which we have covered in a previous chapter.

The Feast of Tabernacles, also called The Feast of Booths, or just Booths, or The Feast of Ingathering (so named for the harvest) is the last Feast of the year and contains the 6ᵗʰ and 7ᵗʰ High Day Sabbaths of the year. The Israelites were required to make a temporary shelter from branches to commemorate the provision of Yahweh in the 40 years of wilderness wanderings.

> *"In the 15th day of the seventh month, WHEN YOU HAVE GATHERED IN THE FRUIT OF THE LAND, you shall keep a feast unto the LORD seven days: on the first day shall be a Sabbath and on the eighth day shall be a Sabbath." Leviticus 23:39.*

Let us review the Feasts of the LORD... they tell a story:

1. Passover... Accept Christ as your savior and let Him plead His Blood on your behalf.
2. Feast of Unleavened Bread... Put away the sinful life and repent.
3. Pentecost... accept the free gift of the Holy Spirit and follow Him.
4. Trumpets... know that God's judgement is near.
5. Atonement... to those who have been covered in the blood of the Lamb (Passover) and have adopted a new and living way (Unleavened Bread) and walked in the Spirit (Pentecost) and WATCHED for the coming of our Savior (Trumpets) know that your salvation is sure by the ATONING sacrifice of Jesus Christ (Atonement).
6. Tabernacles... as born-again believers, we realize that this world is not our home. We are but "pilgrims" upon this earth. This is our temporary dwelling as is our body. For 6 long days (6000 years) this has been the case, but good news is here! The last day of the Feast of Ingathering is the 8th day and is called; THE LAST GREAT DAY... it represents a day that will never end.

The Eighth Day

Numbers play a significant role in creation.

1. The number one denotes commencement and unity.
2. The number two denotes difference. If two people agree in testimony, there is unity, if not, two implies opposition and division as it was in the 2nd day of creation.
3. Three denotes completeness. Also, divine perfection.
4. Four denotes creative works. Four is used in respect to the material world.
5. Five is the number of Grace.

6. Six is the human number. Man works 6 days. Man was created the 6th day.
7. Seven denotes spiritual perfection. Seven regulates every aspect of our lives… Seven days a week, etc.
8. Eight denotes RESURRECTION, REGENERATION, a new beginning or commencement.

Circumcision

The first mention of circumcision in scripture is in Genesis,

> *"This is My Covenant, which you shall keep, between Me and you and your seed after you; Every man child among you shall be circumcised. And you shall circumcise the flesh of your foreskin; and it shall be a TOKEN of the covenant between Me and you. And he that is EIGHT DAYS OLD shall be circumcised among you, every man child in your generations, he that is born in the house, or bought with money of any stranger which is not of your seed." Genesis 17:10-12.*

Under the Old Covenant you see that Abraham was given the law of circumcision which was a "sign" or "token" between God and His people.

Under the New Covenant, Circumcision is still a "sign" or "token" between God and His people but instead of being an outward expression in the flesh it has become an inward reality in the Spirit.

> *"For he is not a Jew, which is one outwardly; neither is that circumcision which is outward in the flesh: But he is a Jew, which is one inwardly; and circumcision is that of the heart, in the spirit, and not in the letter; whose praise*

in not of men, but of God." Romans 2:28-29.

"And I will give them one heart, and I will put a new Spirit within you, and I will take the stony heart out of their flesh and will give them a heart of flesh: That they may walk in My statutes, and keep My ordinances, and do them: and they shall be My people, and I will be their God." Ezekiel 11:19-20.

Paul wrote to the church at Colossae:

"Beware lest any man spoil you through philosophy and vain deceit, after the tradition of men, after the rudiments of the world, and not after Christ. For in Him dwells all the fulness of the Godhead bodily. And you are complete in Him, which is the head of all principality and power: IN WHOM YOU ARE ALSO CIRCUMCISED WITH THE CIRCUMCISION MADE WITHOUT HANDS, in putting off the body of the sins of the flesh by the CIRCUMCISION OF CHRIST." Colossians 2:8-11.

Do you see that Circumcision in the flesh pointed to or was the "type" of the circumcision of the Heart?

So now one must ask the question... What does the 8th day point to?

Answer: The Last Great Day. The 8th day of the Feast of Tabernacles is the 7th (7 denotes spiritual perfection) High Holy Day of the Year. The number 8 denotes a resurrection/regeneration, a NEW BEGINNING or commencement.

Are you starting to see the BIG PICTURE?

Do you see that God is telling the story of salvation through His Feasts? And remember the 7 X 7 = 49 + 1 = 50 formula? It is the same for a Jubilee and for the count to Pentecost. Why? Because the Exodus, The Feast Days, and The Jubilee are all intertwined. They are all telling the story of salvation.

We used the Jubilee to recon the time of the wilderness wandering here on earth in a previous chapter.

We can use the same 7 X 7 = 49 + 1 = 50 formula to recon the time from the pouring out of the "former rain" in 31 CE until the Feast of Trumpets.

How long was Jesus seen alive by His apostles after His resurrection?

Luke gives us the answer:

> *"To whom also He showed Himself alive after His Passion by many infallible proofs, BEING SEEN OF THEM FORTY DAYS, and speaking of the things pertaining to the kingdom of God." Acts 1:3.*

Why 40 Days? Because 40 X 50 = 2000 and 31 CE + 2000 = 2031.

Meditate on what I have written. Educate yourself on the Feasts of the LORD. Ask the Holy Spirit to reveal these things to you.

Jesus Is Coming... Soon!

CHAPTER 18

THE ABOMINATION OF DESOLATION

Jesus knew that His time was drawing near after 3 ½ years of ministry. He was about to give His life as a ransom for mankind. One of the crowning achievements of His ministry besides spreading the gospel message, was His telling the Scribes and Pharisees just what He thought of them. In reading Matthew 23 one can see the utter disdain and contempt that Jesus had for the ruling elite of that time.

He told them that they were "blind guides," that they were to receive "damnation," He called them "hypocrites," "fools," and "serpents." Then He said,

> "Behold, your house is left unto you desolate. For I say to you, you shall not see Me again till you shall say, "Blessed is He that comes in the name of the LORD." Matthew 23:38-39.

No wonder they wanted to kill Him! Jesus told them exactly what they needed to hear. They had the option then, of repentance, or damnation. It is the same for everyone. I choose repentance, how about you?

Jesus then left the Temple and came to His disciples and told them,

"See all these things? (Referring to the Temple complex) I say unto you, there shall not be left here one stone upon another that shall not be thrown down." Matthew 24:2.

His disciples then asked 3 extremely important questions:

1. Tell us, when shall these things be? (Destruction of the Temple)
2. What shall be the sign of Your coming? (2nd coming)
3. And of the end of the world?

Jesus' immediate response was one of warning:

"Take heed that no man deceives you." Matthew 24:4.

Why would that be His very first response to 3 immensely important questions?

Answer: Because He knew that deception is the tool most utilized by the enemy. It is the mixture of truth and lies that the enemy and his ministers use to deceive. See: 2 Corinthians 11:13-15.

The warning is valid today more than ever before.

Jesus then gave His apostles signs to look for: false messiahs, wars, rumors of wars, famines, pestilences, earthquakes in various places, and then He told them that they would be hated for His name's sake. He told them that they would be killed, and that iniquity (lawlessness) would increase, and many would be "offended," and love would "wax cold."

At the time of this writing, (2021) this perfectly describes the current situation. People nowadays are OFFENDED at every little thing. To see that love is waxing cold all one needs to do is turn on a newscast. Children are killing their parents. Parents are killing their children, etc. There is good news though: Jesus said,

"He that shall endure until the end, shall be saved."

"And this gospel of the kingdom shall be preached in all the world for a witness unto all nations; AND THEN SHALL THE END COME."

With the "world wide web" I believe this prophecy is being fulfilled NOW. Don't you? And it is not only the advent of the internet, but also missionaries and local churches bringing the gospel message.

I live in a suburb of Dallas, Texas and work approximately 3 miles from my home. Driving to work a few days ago, I counted the churches that I could see in the 3-mile drive. I counted 12. 12 church buildings in my drive to work. I think that the gospel of the kingdom is being preached in all the world for a witness unto all nations... NOW, at the time of this writing.

After giving the apostles the signs and the good news of Matthew 24:13, and the final sign of the gospel being preached, He declared that the END would come. Then He reverted to giving more "signs" of what to look for:

"When you therefore shall see the ABOMINATION of DESOLATION, spoken of by Daniel the prophet, stand in the holy place, (Whosoever reads, let him understand) then let them which be in Judea flee into the mountains: Let him which is on the housetop not come down to take anything out of his house... For then shall be Great Tribulation, such as was not since the beginning of the world to this time, no, nor ever shall be. And except those days should be shortened, there should no flesh be saved: but for the elect's sake those days shall be shortened." Matthew 24:15-17, 21-22.

Clearly the Abomination of Desolation ushers in the period of Great Tribulation. However, we have already learned in a previous chapter that a "7 Year" Tribulation period is erroneous because the 7 Year period is taken from Daniel 9:27 and separated from the 70-week prophecy... so forget that nonsense.

Turn on the News channel. Look at the Tribulation going on right now.

Let us look at "Great Tribulation" spoken of elsewhere in the Scriptures.

After the sealing of the 144,000 in Revelation 7, John wrote:

> *"After this I beheld, and a great multitude, WHICH NO MAN COULD NUMBER, of all nations, and kindreds, and people, and languages, stood before the throne, and before the Lamb, clothed with white robes and palms in their hands; And cried with a loud voice, saying, "Salvation to our God which sits upon the throne, and unto the Lamb." And all the angels stood round about the throne, and about the elders and the four beasts, and fell before the throne on their faces, and worshipped God, saying, "Amen: Blessing, and glory and wisdom and thanksgiving and honor and power and might be unto our God forever and ever. Amen." And one of the elders answered, saying to me, "What are these which are arrayed in white robes? And from where do they come?" And I said to him, "Sir, you know." And he said to me, "These are they which came out of GREAT TRIBULATION, and have washed their robes, and made them white in the blood of the Lamb." Revelation 7:9-14.*

So, let me ask you this: Do you think that the only people who are going to be saved are the 144,000 and the people who came through the "Great Tribulation" which is yet to come? What about believers from the past 2000 years?

Doesn't it make much more sense to realize that there
has been "Great Tribulation" throughout history?

Anyone who has ever read: "Foxe's Book of Martyrs" first pub-
lished March 20, 1563, cannot deny that "Great Tribulation" has
been occurring throughout history.

However, Jesus did point to a period of Tribulation which is not
universal but specific to a period following the "Abomination of
Desolation" spoken of by Daniel the Prophet. So let us turn our
attention to the book of Daniel and see if we can discover exactly
WHAT or WHO the ABOMINATION OF DESOLATION is.

*"And He shall confirm the covenant with many for one
week: and in the midst of the week, He shall cause the sacrifice and the oblation to cease, and for the overspreading of ABOMINATIONS He shall make it DESOLATE, even
until the consummation, and that determined shall be
poured upon the DESOLATE." Daniel 9:27.*

Jesus is the one who confirmed the "covenant" with many for 1
week (7 years), 3 ½ years of personal ministry and 3 ½ years of
sending His Disciples to the lost sheep of Israel. And didn't Jesus
say to the Jews,

*"Your house (Temple) is left unto you DESO-
LATE?" (Matthew 23:38, Luke 13:35).*

"Even until the consummation," refers to the consummation or
end of the age.

In other words: Because the Jews would not listen to Jesus and
repent and turn back to God, the patience of the LORD ran out
and the Temple was demolished and will remain that way (desolate) until the end of the world as we know it... until the con-

summation of all things (The END).

Do not be fooled into thinking that the Temple will be rebuilt in Jerusalem before the 2nd Advent of our Savior.

God Said It Will Not.

"And arms shall stand on his part, and they shall pollute the sanctuary of strength and shall take away the daily sacrifice, and they shall place the ABOMINATION THAT MAKES DESOLATE." Daniel 11:31.

This passage is referring to Antiochus IV Epiphanes. He erected an altar to ZEUS (Jupiter) upon the altar of burnt offering at the Temple in Jerusalem, among other abominable practices of sacrilege.

After Antiochus conquered Jerusalem, (without a fight) he wanted to "unite" the people by "Hellenization."

"Moreover, king Antiochus wrote to his whole kingdom that all should be one people, and everyone should leave his laws: so, all the heathen agreed according to the commandment of the king. Yes, many also of the Israelites consented to his religion, and sacrificed unto idols, and profaned the sabbath. Now the fifteenth day of the month Chisleu, in the hundred forty and fifth year, they set up THE ABOMINATION OF DESOLATION upon the altar, and builded idol altars throughout the cities of Judah on every side." 1 Maccabees 1:41-43, 54.

"Not long after this the king sent an old man of Athens to compel the Jews to depart from the laws of their fathers,

and not to live after the Laws of God: And to pollute also the Temple in Jerusalem, and to call it the Temple of Jupiter Olympus." 2 Maccabees 6:1-2a.

So, it is a fact of history that Antiochus defiled the Temple and rededicated it to a false god, Zeus or Jupiter, whichever you prefer... the point is:

"The thing that has been, it is that which shall be, and that which is done is that which shall be done; and there is no new thing under the sun. Is there anything whereof it may be said, "See, this is new?" It has been already of old time, which was before us." Ecclesiastes 1:9-10.

In other words, Jesus said the Abomination of Desolation would "STAND IN THE HOLY PLACE" (Matthew 24:15) so what is "STANDING" in the Holy Place Now?

The Dome Of The Rock.

Think about it. Antiochus rededicated the Temple to Zeus, and Islam built a shrine to "ALLAH."

What is the difference? Solomon said that there is no new thing under the sun! The names and other factors may change but the same thing keeps happening repeatedly.

The Temple Mount is where Abraham was willing to sacrifice his son Isaac, making the site holy to Christians, Jews, and Muslims. Islam says that it is also the site where Muhammed ascended to heaven.

Here is something to ponder: If the Koran says that Jesus is not the Son of God (Surah 18), and the Christian bible says that anyone who denies that Jesus is the Son of God is the ANTICHRIST (1 & 2 John) then wouldn't that make Muhammed the "FALSE

PROPHET" of the Christian Bible? (Revelation 19 & 20).

And, if all of that is true (which it is) then wouldn't the Dome of the Rock fulfill the Abomination of Desolation requirement of Matthew 24:15? (And Mark 13:14 & Luke 21:24b).

The Abomination of Desolation today, standing in the Holy Place, Is the DOME OF THE ROCK.

Jesus Is Coming… Soon.

CHAPTER 19

SAVING THE BEST FOR LAST

T he return of Jesus to the planet Earth has been antici-
pated since 31 AD. The apostles asked Him just before He
ascended into heaven,

> *"Lord, will you at this time restore again the kingdom to
> Israel?" Acts 1:6b.*

It was a valid question. They still expected the Messiah to thwart
Roman rule and vanquish their enemies. Jesus' response to the
question was this:

> *"It is not for YOU to know the times or the seasons, which
> the Father has put in His own power. But you shall receive
> power, after the Holy Ghost is come upon you; and you
> shall be witnesses unto Me both in Jerusalem, and in all
> Judea, and in Samaria, and unto the uttermost part of
> the earth." Acts 1:7b-8.*

In other words, Jesus was saying, hey guys, do not worry about
when I will return, it will not be in your lifetime, your focus
needs to be on spreading the good news (gospel) once you have
received the Holy Spirit. That is your job.

My personal thoughts are that Jesus was vague about the time of His return on purpose so that believers in the gospel would continue in the faith and not become lackadaisical in their walk with Him.

It is this vagueness that has led some "theologians" to postulate that Jesus really does not have any idea about the time period allotted for His return. This is a mistake. For those who take that stance, I pose this question:

Do you really think that a demon knows more about the time period allotted or for the "dispensation" in question than Jesus Himself?

Remember the demoniac asking Jesus,

> *"Have you come here to torment us BEFORE THE TIME?"*
> *Matthew 8:29b*

THE DEMON KNEW THAT HE WAS 2000 YEARS EARLY.

The mistake that "theologians" make is that they misinterpret the words:

> *"No one knows the day or the hour"*

to mean that there is not a time period allotted. This is a mistake as well. There is a DAY Appointed for All Things under the Sun. God is highly organized. He knows the END of all things from the BEGINNING.

In Fact, Jesus Is The Beginning And The End.

To think that the demons know more about the time period allotted for Christ's return than Christ himself is simply ludicrous.

No one knows the DAY OR THE HOUR not the demons, not Jesus, only the Father... But, nowhere in Scripture does it say that no one can know the YEAR of the time allotted, (time period of the "church dispensation").

In fact, just the opposite is true. We have already explored the many ways of reckoning the "Determined" time of His Visitation and for the VERY BEST example of scripture showing us this time period, the wait is over, we will discover this AMAZING prophecy now.

Some setup is required before revealing this chilling prophecy...

> "And I saw in the right hand of Him that sat on the throne a book written within and on the backside, sealed with seven seals. And I saw a strong angel proclaiming with a loud voice, "Who is worthy to open the book, and to loosen the seals thereof?" And no man in heaven, nor in earth, neither under the earth, was able to open the book, neither to look thereon. And I wept much, because no man was found worthy to open and to read the book, neither to look thereon. And one of the elders said unto me, "Weep not: behold, the LION of the tribe of JUDAH, the ROOT of DAVID, has prevailed to open the book, and to loosen the seven seals thereof." Revelation 5:1-5.

Who is it that is worthy to open the seals? Who is of the root of David? The tribe of Judah?

It Is Jesus.

Keep in mind that the Lion is Jesus.

> "For I will be unto Ephraim as a LION and as a young lion to the house of Judah: I, even I, will tear and GO AWAY; I will take away, and none shall rescue him. I will GO AND RETURN to My place, until they acknowledge their

*offence and seek My face: in their affliction they will seek
Me early, Come, and let us RETURN to the LORD: for He
has torn, and He WILL HEAL US; He has smitten, and He
will BIND US UP.*

*AFTER TWO DAYS WILL HE REVIVE US: IN THE THIRD
DAY HE WILL RAISE US UP, AND WE SHALL LIVE IN
HIS SIGHT.*

*Then shall we know, if we follow on to know the LORD:
His GOING FORTH is PREPARED as the morning; and
He shall come unto us as the rain, as the LATTER AND
FORMER RAIN unto the earth." Hosea 5:14-6:3.*

Wow! Amazing!

This passage of scripture is what Peter had in mind as he spoke
of the 2nd coming of Jesus... How do I know? Because the Holy
Spirit told me that he was thinking of this passage when he gave
us the formula: 1 Day = 1 Thousand Years and 1 Thousand Years
= 1 Day.

Peter was writing about the 2nd coming and the Spirit reminded
him of this passage that I capitalized above, and that is when he
wrote to

"Not be ignorant of THIS ONE THING..."

*"This second epistle, beloved, I now write unto you; in
both which I stir up your pure minds by way of remem-*

brance; that you may be mindful of the words which were spoken before by the holy prophets (especially Hosea), and of the commandment of us the apostles of the Lord and Savior: Knowing this first, that there shall come in THE LAST DAYS SCOFFERS, walking after their own lusts, and saying, "Where is the PROMISE of HIS COMING? For since the fathers died, all things continue as they were from the beginning of creation." For this they willingly are ignorant of, that by the Word of God the heavens were of old , and the earth standing out of the water and in the water: Whereby the world that then was being overflowed with water, Perished: But the heavens and the earth, which are now, by the same word are kept in store, RESERVED UNTO FIRE AGAINST THE DAY OF JUDGMENT and perdition of ungodly men. But beloved, BE NOT IGNORANT OF THIS ONE THING!!!!!

That One Day Is With The Lord As A Thousand Years, And A Thousand Years As One Day.

The Lord is not slack concerning His Promise (2nd coming) as some men count slackness; but is longsuffering to us, not willing that any should perish but that ALL SHOULD COME TO REPENTANCE. But the DAY OF THE LORD will come as a thief in the night (to those who are unprepared See: 1 Thess. 5:4) in which the heavens shall pass away with a great noise and the ELEMENTS shall melt with fervent heat, the earth also and the works that are therein shall be burned up. Seeing then that all these things shall be dissolved, what manner of persons ought you to be in all holy conversation and godliness, looking for and hasting unto the coming of the day of God wherein the heavens being on fire shall be dissolved,

and the elements shall melt with fervent heat?" 2 Peter
3:1-12.

Do you know what is made of "elements?"

EVERYTHING. ALL MATTER IS MADE UP OF ELEMENTS.

The Heavens being on fire shall be DISSOLVED.

The Sun will go "SUPERNOVA!"

The Moon will be as bright as the Sun!

> *"And there shall be upon every high mountain, and upon*
> *every high hill, rivers and streams of waters in the day*
> *of the great slaughter, WHEN THE TOWERS FALL. More-*
> *over, the light of the moon shall be as the light of the sun*
> *and the light of the sun shall be seven-fold as the light of*
> *seven days (like the furnace of Daniel 3:19b) in the day*
> *that the LORD binds up the breach of His people and heals*
> *the stroke of their wound. Behold, the name of the LORD*
> *comes from far, burning with His anger, and the burden*
> *thereof is heavy: His lips are full of indignation, and His*
> *tongue as a devouring fire." Isaiah 30:25-27.*

Do you see the urgency and severity of turning to God to escape what is soon to come upon the earth?

Hosea said,

"AFTER TWO DAYS HE WILL REVIVE US."

In other words, Jesus was crucified in 31 AD and 2000 years added to 31 brings us to 2031 as the year that has been "determined." Remember though, that the time period will be shortened for the elect's sake. (Matthew 24:22).

Hosea also said,

*"IN THE THIRD DAY HE WILL RAISE US UP AND WE
SHALL LIVE IN HIS SIGHT."*

The end of the second day is swiftly approaching and when Jesus
descends from heaven it will close and the third day will dawn.

> *"For the Lord Himself shall descend from heaven with
> a SHOUT, with the voice of the archangel, and with
> the TRUMPET of God: and the dead in Christ SHALL
> RISE first: then we which are alive and remain shall be
> CAUGHT UP together with them in the clouds to meet
> the Lord IN THE AIR: and so, shall we ever be with the
> Lord." (Living in His sight). 1 Thessalonians 4:16-17.*

The new day will dawn. Will you be there?

In The Third Day

He Will Raise Us Up

And We Shall Live In His Sight

And So Shall We Ever Be With The Lord

EPILOGUE

"For the kingdom of heaven is like a man that is a house-holder, who went out early in the morning to hire laborers into his vineyard. And when he had agreed with the laborers for a penny a day, he sent them into his vineyard. And he went out about the third hour (9 AM) and saw others standing idle in the marketplace and said to them: "Go you also into the vineyard and whatsoever is right I will give you." And they went their way. Again, he went out about the sixth (12 noon) and ninth hour (3 PM) and did likewise. And about the ELEVENTH HOUR (5 PM) he went out, and found others standing idle and said to them, "Why do you stand here all day idle?" They said to him, "Because no man has hired us." He said to them, "Go you also into the vineyard; and whatsoever is right that shall you receive." So, when evening was come, the lord of the vineyard said to his steward, "Call the laborer's and give them their hire, beginning from the last unto the first." And when they came that were hired about the eleventh hour, they received every man a penny. But when the first came, they supposed that they should have received more; and they likewise received every man a penny. And when they had received it, they murmured against the goodman of the house, saying, "These last have worked only one hour, and you have made them equal to us, which have borne the burden and heat of the day." But he answered one of them and said, "Friend, I do you no wrong, did you not agree with me for a penny? Take what

is yours and go your way: I will give to the last, even as unto you. Is it not lawful for me to do what I will with my own? Is your eye evil because I am good? So, the last shall be first, and the first last: for many are called, but few chosen." Matthew 20:1-16.

It Is The Eleventh Hour My Friends.

Have you accepted the invitation to work in the Lord's vineyard?

It does not matter that the day is far spent. He will give you your wages.

We all have wages, and we all serve a master...

"Don't you know that to whom you yield yourselves servants to obey, his servants you are to whom you obey, whether of sin unto death, or of obedience unto righteousness? For the wages of sin is death, but the gift of God is eternal life through Jesus Christ our Lord." Romans 6:16,23.

It does not matter that it is the eleventh hour. God will give YOU the same free gift of ETERNAL LIFE that He has given someone who has been saved since childhood.

God will give you the same gift of eternal life as He gave Billy Graham recently.

Before Mr. Graham passed, He said, "If someone tells you that Billy Graham has died, DON'T YOU BELIEVE IT! For I have never been so ALIVE!"

Death is only scary for lost souls who will spend eternity in outer darkness separated from God.

If you have never invited Christ into your heart, just say this simple prayer and mean it:

> *"Jesus, I am sorry for all my sins. I realize that I am a sinner and I invite you now to become the Lord of my life. Please forgive me and help me to live for you... Amen."*

If you prayed that prayer, the next step is to be baptized and ask the Holy Spirit to come into your heart and guide you.

Read your bible daily.

Try to find a suitable church to attend as the Spirit leads you.

> *"And the Spirit and the bride say, Come. And let him that hears say, Come. And let him that is thirsty, Come. And whosoever will, let him take the water of life freely."* Revelation 22:17.

The End

Amen